Geometric Design in Weaving

Else Regensteiner

Manifesting Word. Tapestry by Stephen Thurston. (Photo courtesy of Stephen Thurston).

Jacket photo:
Weaving by Philip E. Smith. (Photo by Patricia Lambert)

Printed in the United States of America.
ISBN: 0-88640-078-7
Published by Schiffer Publishing Ltd.
1469 Morstein Road, West Chester, Pennsylvania 19380

This book may be purchased from the publisher.
Please include $1.50 postage.
Try your bookstore first.

Acknowledgments

This book could not have been accomplished without the active assistance and participation of my artistic and knowledgeable friends and associates. Sincere thanks are given to the many textile artists across the nation who freely shared their work, skill, and experience in photographs and directions.

My heartfelt thanks and deep appreciation are extended to: Irene and George Suyeoka, who not only contributed excellent drawings, weavings, diagrams, and photographs, but also their valuable time, enthusiasm, and encouragement; to Judith Gordon, whose complex weave analysis, painstaking drafting, competent advice, and final typing of the manuscript were invaluable components of this book; to Sadye Tune Wilson, whose expertise and design abilities enriched the sections on "Dynamic Symmetry" and "Tessellation"; to Hector Garcia, Bernard Gordon, and George Suyeoka special thanks for their wonderful photography.

I gratefully acknowledge the cooperation of Maebetty Langdon and of Christa C. Mayer Thurman, curator of textiles at The Art Institute of Chicago, who, together with Cynthia J. Cannon, allowed us to select photographs and peruse precious textiles from their collections.

I thank my husband for his continued patience and kindness.

Last, but not least, I sincerely thank Irene Demchyshyn for the skill and understanding with which she edited the manuscript.

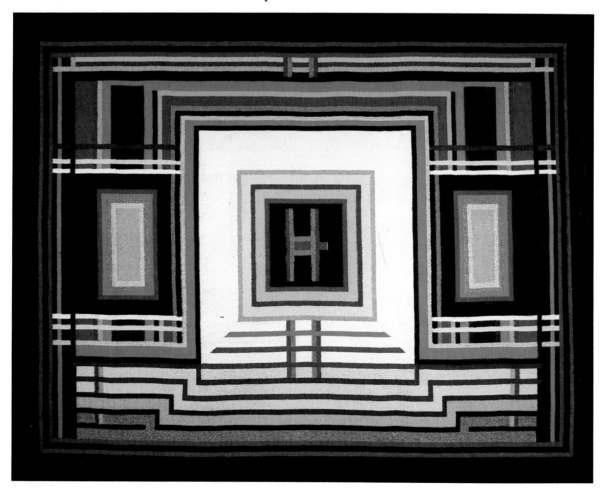

Geometric Tapestry I   by Stephen Thurston. (Photo courtesy of Stephen Thurston).

Contents

Star in the Sky, double weave by Peter Townley.
(Photo courtesy of Peter Townley).

Butterflies, tapestry by Gloria Mae Campbell. (Photo courtesy of Gloria Mae Campbell).

Detail of *Butterflies* by Gloria Mae Campbell. (Photo courtesy of Gloria Mae Campbell).

Introduction

My intention in writing this book was to explore the possibilities of geometric design from the weaver's and artist's point of view. I have treated theory and design systems and devices as well as the range of basic shapes in the context of visual presentation and technical execution. The weaver and textile artist will find abstract shapes most valuable and, I hope, will gain inspiration, stimulation, and awareness from their transformation into double weaves, pattern weaves, tapestries, rugs, and hangings.

In an effort to make the weaver aware of the many shapes and their possibilities and potentials as an incentive to the successful designing of beautiful textiles, I have organized *Geometric Design in Weaving* as follows:

Chapter 1 acquaints the reader with basic shapes, their relationships and variations. Chapter 2 explains the many ways in which drawings, cut-out paper and collages can be used for experimentation and as an aid in visualizing the effect the woven textile will present. Various methods suggest creative approaches that can be used to help the weaver select the right technique before final decisions are made. Assemblage of materials and construction of a tactile chart both further sensitivity for the feel and qualities of a great variety of materials and textures.

Chapter 3 presents designs selected for their special interest and significance from the standpoint of their historic development and use through the ages, as well as for the beauty and versatility with which they can be applied in many woven interpretations. Meander, Paisley, and the Chilkat blanket are extensively explored within this context.

Monterey Night Melody, by Patricia Kreider. (Photo courtesy of Patricia Kreider)

One of the most fascinating aspects of design lies in the arrangement of proportions. Mathematicians and scientists have studied laws of symmetry and proportion in nature for many centuries and have transposed them into formulas that are employed by architects, painters, textile and graphic designers, and many of the most accomplished weavers. Chapter 4 deals with such systems of design and proportion. Its study can open new vistas for weavers who need to arrange surface divisions for place mats and pillow tops, rugs, tapestries, wall hangings, or clothing.

Chapters 5 and 6 present technical methods of rug and tapestry weaving and show many beautiful examples of ancient and contemporary origin for design inspiration. Chapter 7 concentrates on weaver-controlled methods of laid-in, pick-up, and double weaves and also explores the unusual technique of Karelian Red Pick.

For the weaver with 4- or multi-harness looms, chapters 8 and 9 offer many loom-controlled weaves and patterns. Name drafts, block weaves, damasks, and supplementary warps are explained with explicit drafts and drawings. Loom-controlled double weaves and three-dimensional structures are presented in great variety in Chapter 10.

I have tried to present drafts, diagrams, and explanations as thoroughly and clearly as possible so that the reader will not have to keep referring to other books. In order to do this, I have inevitably had to include an explanation of drafting; some diagrams used in the text may look familiar to readers of my previous books as well. Although the techniques have stayed the same, however, their application to the works of art and design are new, different, and creative. Only the design makes a technique come alive and lifts it from the realm of mere constructivism into the lofty fields of art and function.

Detail of name draft, designed and woven by Eleanor Best. See also fig. 8-8.

Notations.

Comparing the various systems of drafting found in weaving books, I am convinced that the method I have used in my previous publications is still valid and easy to read. The drafts are read in the same way that the weaver follows them on the loom and therefore seem to be the logical graphic presentation.

Threadings are written from left to right. Numbers are used to indicate the harness through which a warp thread runs (a in figure I-1). Directions of threadings can, of course, be reversed if preferred. Filled-in (black) squares in the pattern draw-down (d in the same figure) represent warp threads that are raised. All drafts are written for the rising-shed loom, unless otherwise indicated.

The tie-ups (b in figure I-1) can be reversed for the sinking shed or counterbalanced loom by tying the opposite harnesses to the treadles. When harnesses 2 and 4 are pulled down, the result is the same as if 1 and 3 were raised. Patterns and treadlings are read from the bottom line up.

Color notations are given in the drafts either by symbols or by letters. Keys for notations are placed next to the individual drafts. If variations in symbols are used, they are explained next to the respective drafts. When large designs are planned, as for rugs, upholstery, or coverlets, each filled-out square of the graph paper may represent inches or complete threading units instead of the individual threads in the heddles. These diagrams are called short, or profile, drafts because they represent only the relative width of each pattern block or threading unit. Profile drafts are discussed in chapter 8.

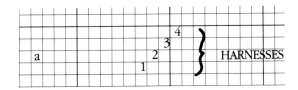

a. threading in the heddles

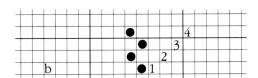

b. tie-up for rising shed loom

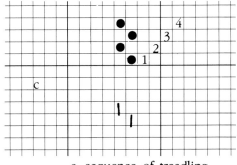

c. sequence of treadling

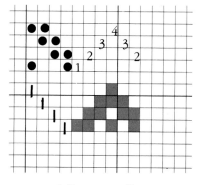

d. pattern in plain weave

e. 2/2 point twill

I-1. Notations for drafting.

Palette. Woven rug by David Cress. (Photo courtesy of David Cress).

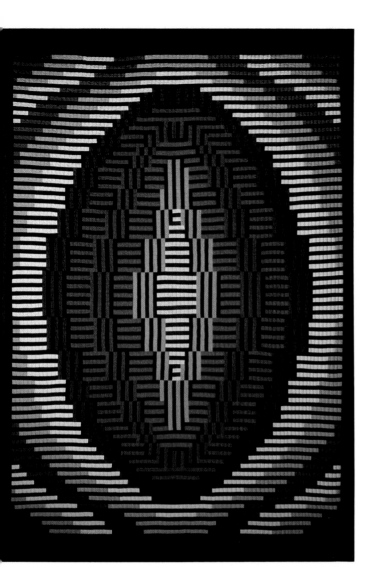

Part I

Design

Burning Bush. Wallhanging by David Cress. (Photo courtesy of David Cress).

Tufted Rug by David Cress. (Photo courtesy of David Cress).

1-1. *Still Life,* by Pablo Picasso. (Photo courtesy of The Art Institute of Chicago)

1-2. *Personages with Star,* by Joan Miro. (Photo courtesy of The Art Institute of Chicago)

Chapter 1

Design Shapes

There is a wealth of geometric designs and shapes suitable for interpretation in textiles. The term geometric, however, conjures up visions of high school mathematics classes, where, with ruler and compass, one learned logical relationships of forms and sizes.

I never appreciated the science of geometry as such, but I always found the visual beauty of orderly arrangements striking and the interaction of forms and shapes, spaces and proportions, fascinating. In time, I became aware of the wonderful symmetry in the stable and dynamic systems that are ever-present in nature and in art.

Geometric forms, as a basis of design, are applied by every artist in endless combinations, may he or she be a painter, sculptor, architect, or weaver. It was Voltaire who stated, "There is a hidden geometry in all the arts the hand produced". Lines define spaces and lead the eye to points of interest; intricate geometric com-

positions evolve from squares, rectangles, circles, triangles, and hexagons. The weaver uses these basic shapes to express ideas in woven forms, be they functional, decorative, conceptional, sculptural, realistic, or abstract.

Combinations of shapes may form the content of the principal figure, as seen in compositions by Picasso, Miro, or Gris; or they may stand on their own, as demonstrated by Piet Mondrian or Josef Hoffman. They may be repetitive, as used by Jack Lenor Larsen; or present theme and variations, as shown in the designs of oriental rugs.

While color and texture play a major role in woven textiles, the emphasis in this book is on structure as such. Color illustrations, however, are included to show how basic geometric shapes are enhanced, changed, softened, or blurred by the influence of color and texture.

Triangulations II, rug in blue composition by Philip E. Smith.
(Photo by Patricia Lambert)

Gradation I. Meet-Cross-and-Separate technique by Marilyn Emerson Holtzer. (Photo courtesy of Marilyn Emerson Holtzer).

Basic Shapes and Variations

Geometric designs consist of arrangements of basic shapes in simple or intricate compositions. Basic shapes are formed by lines in horizontal, vertical, or diagonal directions and are in themselves tools for expression. The principal shapes are: squares, rectangles, diamonds, triangles, circles, ogees, hexagons, and octagons, as well as their many variations and combinations (figs. 1-3 through 1-14).

The sensitive artist can find special expressions in geometric shapes:
- The square is staid and sturdy.
- Rectangles are solid, used to build walls.
- The diamond is decorative and useful, slender or broad, versatile in allover as well as center designs.
- The triangle is more active, more expressive than the rectangle, suggestive of mountaintops and congenial intermingling.
- The circle is light and airy, floating like a balloon.
- The ogee is elegant, pompous, and fluid, conjuring up visions of velvets and damasks.
- Horizontal lines in well-balanced proportions have significance and can show stability and strength.
- Vertical lines can be arranged in static or dynamic ways, even or uneven, and emphasize height and slender reach.

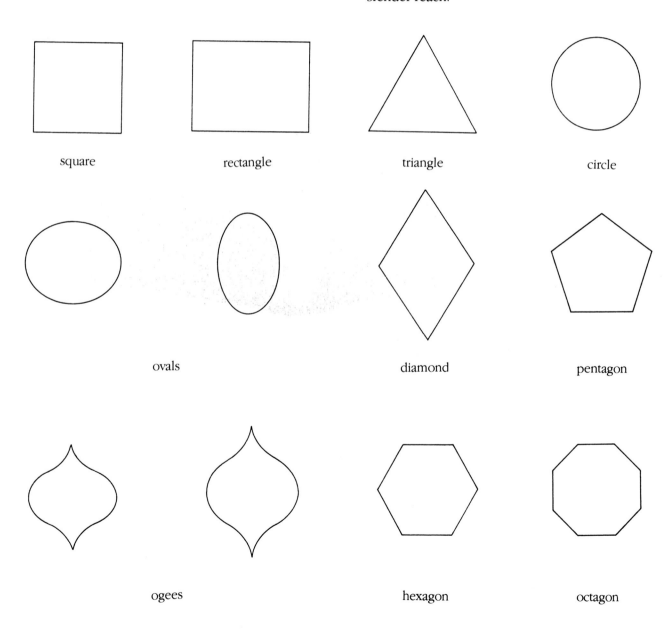

square   rectangle   triangle   circle

ovals   diamond   pentagon

ogees   hexagon   octagon

1-3. Basic shapes   (Drawings by George Suyeoka)

1-4. Square variations.

1-5. Rectangle variations.

1-6. Triangle variations.

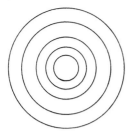
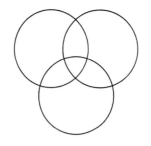
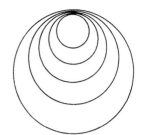

1-7. Circle variations.

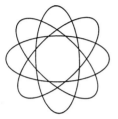
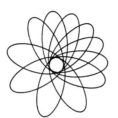
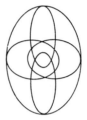
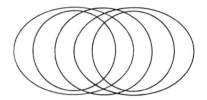

1-8. Oval variations.

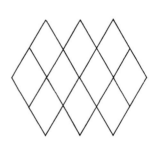

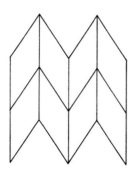
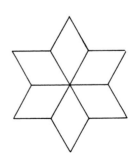

1-9. Diamond variations.

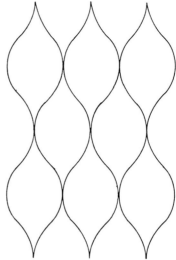

1-10. Ogee variations.

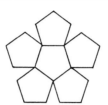

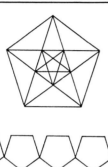
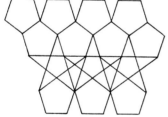

1-11. Pentagon variations.

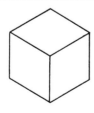
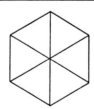

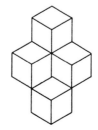
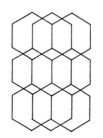
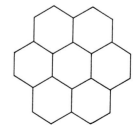

1-12. Hexagon variations.

19

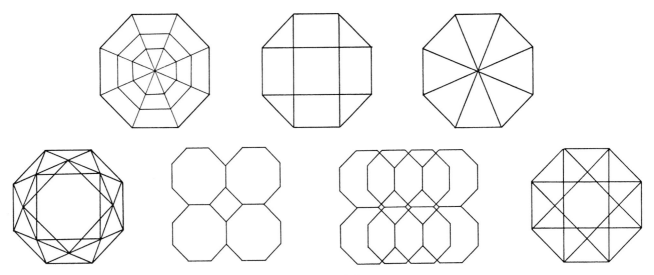

1-13. Octagon variations.

horizontal lines

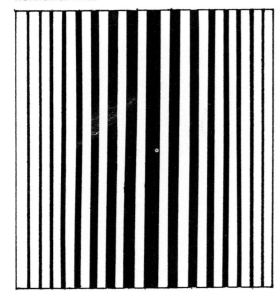

vertical lines

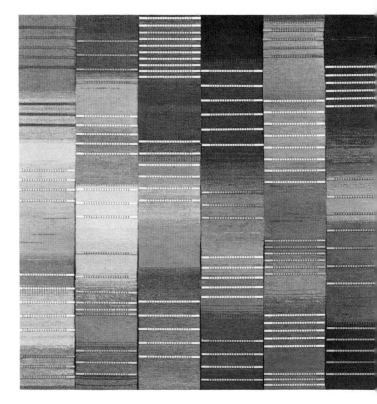

1-14. Lines

Proportions and the placement of shapes also play a major role and can make the difference in the quality and value of a design. Since earliest times, architects have found their basic conceptions in ancient rules and have used them for their structure of buildings and for shapes of doors, windows, and pillars.

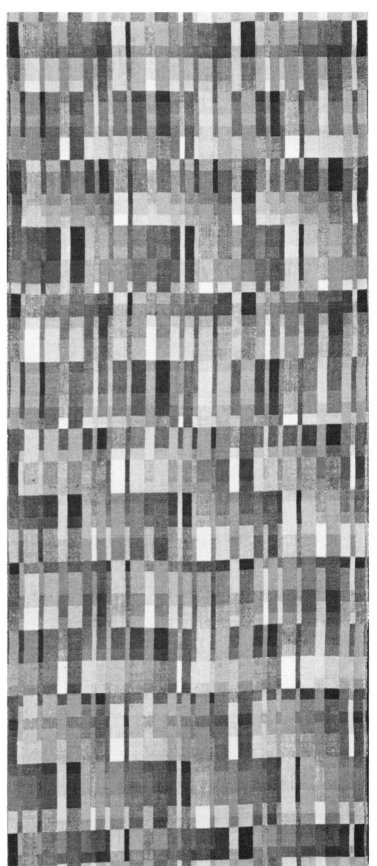

1-15. *Wall No. 5,* by Helen Frances Gregor. (Photo courtesy of Helen Frances Gregor)

1-16. *Split Entry 1969,* by Richard Landis. (Courtesy of The Art Institute of Chicago)

1-17. *Urbana I,* serigraph by Louis N. Donato. (Photo courtesy of *Interior Design* magazine)

1-18. *Kleinstadt,* etching by Lyonel Feininger. (Collection of the author; photo by Hector Garcia)

Exciting architectural abstractions and the beauty of city and towns have been interpreted by some of the finest graphic artists. Louis N. Donato describes his serigraph Urbana I (fig. 1-17) as "rooted in abstraction and concerned with shapes, movements, and color on a two-dimensional plane". Lyonel Feininger's "Kleinstadt" (fig. 1-18) shows geometric designs in doors and windows, steeples and the sky, while Paul Klee's whimsical "Witch with the Comb" (fig. 1-19) makes use of delightful circles, dots, lines, and triangles in the human figure.

Other artists, Miro, Juan Gris, Picasso, and Mondrian, for example, and the inventive architect and painter Le Corbusier have combined lines, circles, rectangles, and many other shapes into paintings that are convincing and alive. Their masterworks are vivid proof that geometric figures can fully express an artist's ideas and intentions.

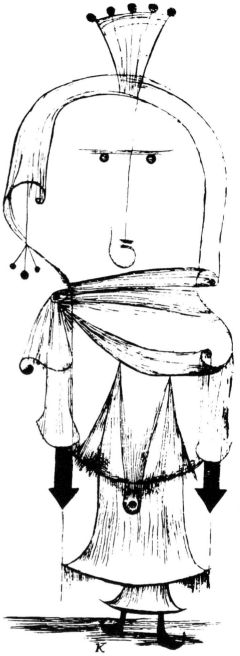

1-20. *The Checkerboard,* oil on canvas by Juan Gris. (Courtesy of the Art Institute of Chicago)

1-19. *The Witch with the Comb,* etching by Paul Klee. (Collection of the author; photo by Hector Garcia)

23

1-21. *Abstract Composition,* oil on canvas by Le Corbusier. (Courtesy of The Art Institute of Chicago)

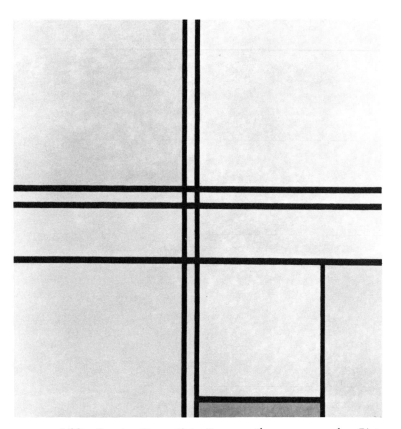

1-22. *Composition—Gris Rouge,* oil on canvas by Piet Mondrian. (Courtesy of The Art Institute of Chicago)

1-23. *Santa Sofia,* silkscreened panel of design by Josef Hoffman. (Courtesy of The Art Institute of Chicago)

Themes and variations of geometric forms have also been used for silk screen prints. One example is the panel shown in figure 1-25. Designed by Frank Lloyd Wright, it is printed on silk and Fortisan in free-floating circles and half circles.

Geometric shapes can also become creative inspirations for the textile artist and weaver. The loom, by its very nature, produces two-dimensional designs and makes geometric compositions attractive in loom-controlled and weaver-controlled methods and techniques. Figures 1-26 through 1-32 show just a few examples of the never-ending variety of squares, grids, hexagons, triangles, and other geometric forms that have been used by textile artists to create woven fabrics of beauty and impact.

1-24. *Panel, Design 506,* Taliesin line of decorative fabrics and wallpapers, designed by Frank Lloyd Wright. (Courtesy of The Art Institute of Chicago)

1-25. *Panel, Design 104,* Taliesin line of decorative fabrics and wallpapers, designed by Frank Lloyd Wright. (Courtesy of The Art Institute of Chicago)

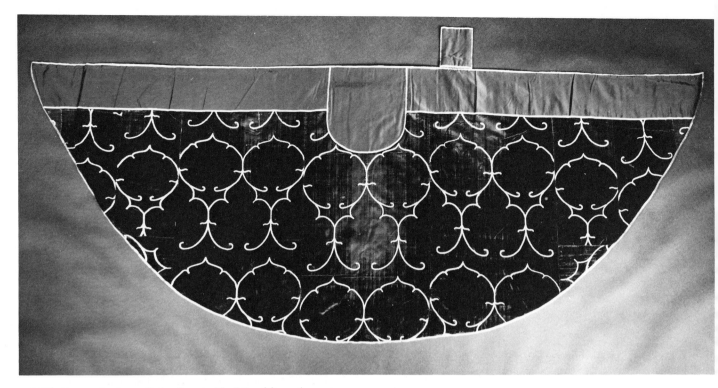

1-26. Cope, Spain or Italy, first half of the fifteenth century. (Courtesy of The Art Institute of Chicago)

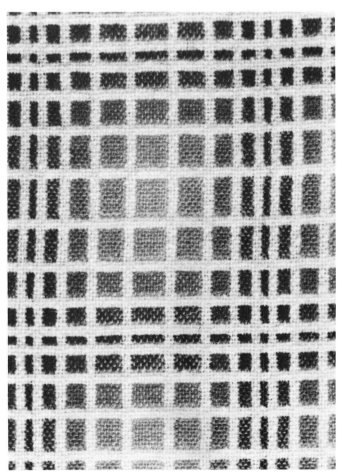

1-27. Double weave fabric, designed by Jack Lenor Larsen. (Photo courtesy of Jack Lenor Larsen)

1-28. *Horsetail,* by Jack Lenor Larsen. (Photo courtesy of Jack Lenor Larsen)

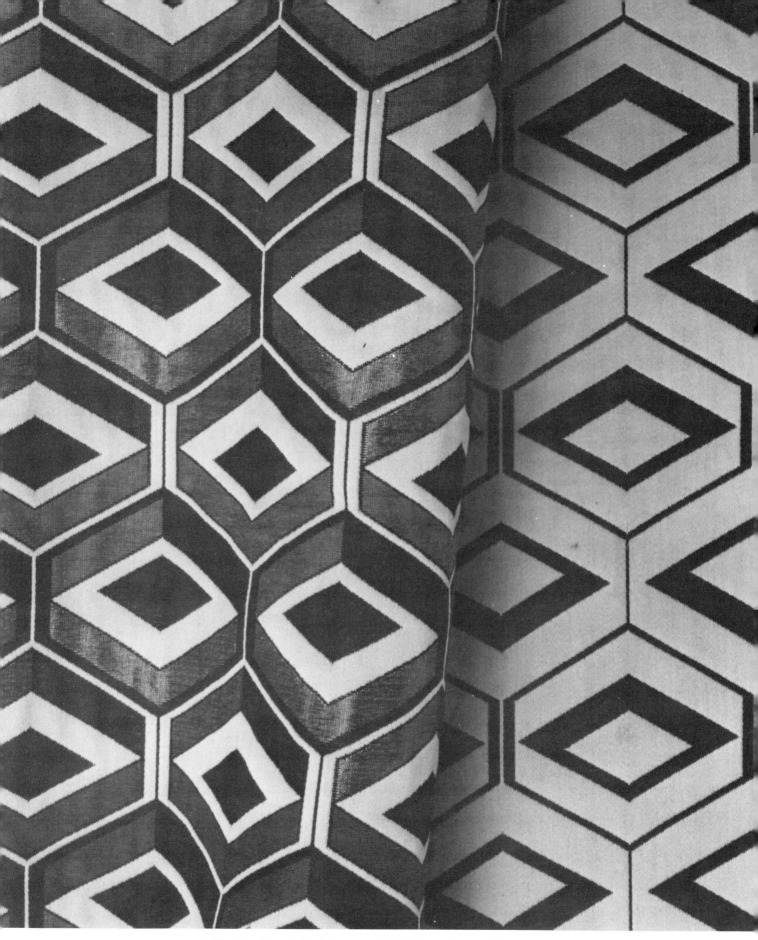

1-29. *Houdini,* triple cloth weave by Jack Lenor Larsen. (Photo by Doris Quarella, courtesy of Jack Lenor Larsen)

1-30. *Woven Design,* by Jane Busse. (Photo courtesy of Jane Busse)

1-31. *Vertical Arrangement,* by Jane Busse. (Photo courtesy of Jane Busse)

1-32. *Fish and Fishes,* by Jane Busse. (Photo courtesy of Jane Busse)

Chapter 2

Design Devices

Multiple variations and expansions of shapes and lines are available to the weaver; each exploration is exciting and rewarding. Many devices for designing have proven easy and effective. It is wise for the weaver to experiment with paper and scissors, pencils and strings, fabrics and fibers, leaves and wood, in order to get a feeling for the effect desired. Textural qualities can be expressed without the benefit of color by the use of corrugated paper and unspun fibers.

Tactile Chart

Exercises originating with the Bauhaus concept emphasize the awareness and fingertip sensitivity that is so important for the textile artist. One such exercise is the tactile chart (fig. 2-1). With no regard to any aspect of the material except its tactile quality, arrange on cardboard pieces of textures ranging from rough to smooth and from warm to cold. The transition may go gradually from the roughest steelwool and sandpaper to the softest velvet and fur, from the warmth of mohair to the coldness of mirror and glass. Not only will you gain visual awareness by practicing this exercise, but when you run your fingers over the surface, keeping your eyes closed, you will also experience the concept of contrast and gradation in its purest tactile form. This sensation adds an exciting new dimension to the designing of geometric shapes.

2-1. Tactile chart. (Photo by George Suyeoka)

Cut Out Paper

Cutting shapes out of black paper and pasting these on a white background (or vice versa) is an excellent way to achieve and observe geometric design (fig. 2-2). You can arrange and rearrange many forms and shapes a dozen times to create the most satisfactory design before you secure the shapes to the background with paste or glue. You can also first draw possible outlines, with pen and then fill these in with cut shapes (fig. 2-3 through 2-7). To achieve transparent effects use thin gray paper and overlap the shapes (fig. 2-8).

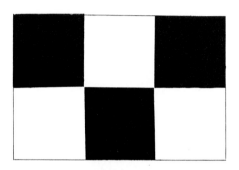

checkerboard

double triangle

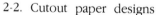

2-2. Cutout paper designs

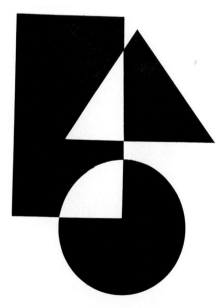

2-3. Design with basic shapes on white paper by Kathleen O'Neal.

2-4. Design with basic shapes as figure-ground design by Kathleen O'Neal.

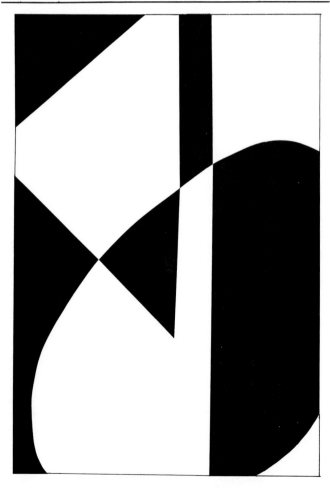

2-5. Cutout paper composition by Connie Peterson.

30

a

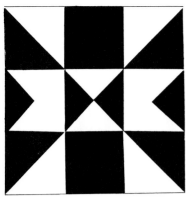

filled in spaces

b

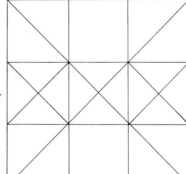

same line design with spaces left empty

motif

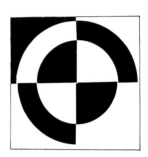

c

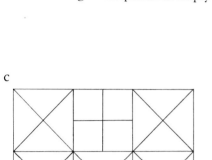

variation with additional lines

d

Squares within squares
line design by Marianita
Porterfield.

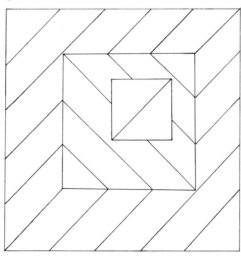

2-6. Skeleton design in three variations by Else Regensteiner.
line design by Marianita Porterfield.

2-7. Broken circles by Irene Suyeoka

2-8. Circles with transparencies by Irene Suyeoka.

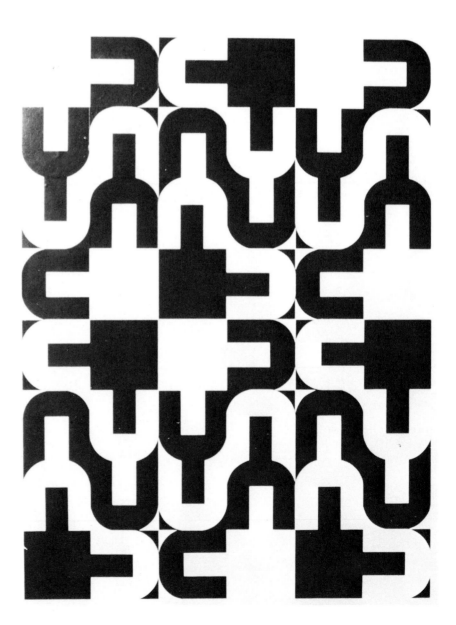

2-9. Figure-background design by Jane Redman. (Photo courtesy of Jane Redman)

2-10. *Abstracted Landscape,* composition with triangles, lines, and circle by Susan Anderson. (Photo courtesy of Jane Redman)

When patterns and background are distributed equally, an optical illusion may occur (fig. 2-9): the design or the background spaces may come forward alternately, and either one may act as the active figure part.

Figures 2-10 and 2-11 show two examples of designing with cutout paper. Susan Anderson's *Abstracted Landscape* is composed of triangles, horizontal lines, and a circle, with the latter acting as the design's point of interest. Although this composition is in black and white, the smaller and diminishing lines blend together to create a third value and the upper part of the design appears to be gray. Actual shades of gray and black paper were used to give transparency and an overlapping sensation to Irene Suyeoka's ogee shapes (fig. 2-11). Their flowing lines illustrate the subtle variations possible in even the most uncomplicated designs.

2-11. Ogee design in three shades by Irene Suyeoka. (Photo by George Suyeoka)

Collages

Collages consist of various materials assembled and placed on a background. This method offers untold numbers of combinations and, limited only by the artist's imagination, adds variety and dimension to the geometric design. Figure 2-12 shows simple shapes of corrugated paper arranged in horizontal, vertical, and diagonal stripes, with two triangles balanced by a circle in the larger one. Textural and visual variations of cloth compose the design of figure 2-13, while twisted silk yarns are used to make a fanlike decorative pattern in fig. 2-14. *Collage* (fig. 2-15) combines circles with other shapes in pink paper on white background, transferring background into design. Fine cotton yarns, meandering in and out of the spaces, give the design interest and fluidity.

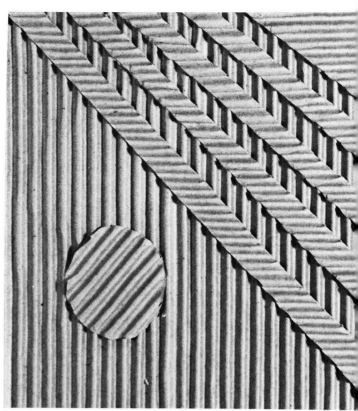

2-12. Corrugated paper collage by Marianita Porterfield. (Photo by George Suyeoka)

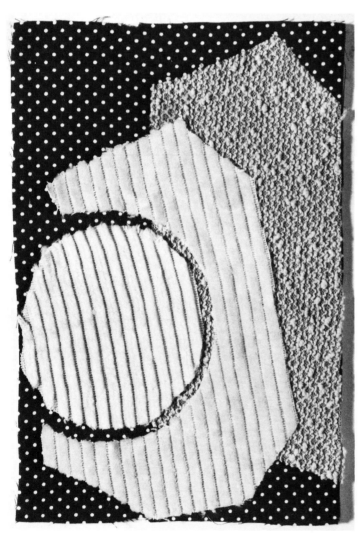

2-13. Fabric collage by Connie Peterson. (Photo by George Suyeoka)

2-14. Yarn collage by Barbara Gent; white cotton yarns on blue and green background. (Photo by George Suyeoka)

Sources of Inspiration for Designs

Once we begin using our eyes to analyze objects, large or small, natural or man-made, we realize that our world consists of arrangements of shapes, lines, and forms that can be separated from each other. Natural forms yield a multitude of basic design combinations. Their relationship of size, shape, proportion, harmony, and contrast are always correct. Challenge and excitement come with the conscious realization of the many choices—simple or complicated, large or small, colorful or monochromatic, smooth or rough, soft or hard—that are on hand for the weaver's imagination and expression.

The perceptive weaver must learn to see. When conscious effort is made to look at everything as a potential source of design, even the most banal encounter becomes significant. An arrangement of leaves or flowers, the wall of a building, a grouping of stones, an iron gate in a wall, or even a woodpile stacked against a house can be retained in the weaver's mind, to be remembered whenever creative ideas are needed.

2-16. Grid in wool yarns over collage of painted paper chips by Marianita Porterfield. (Photo by George Suyeoka)

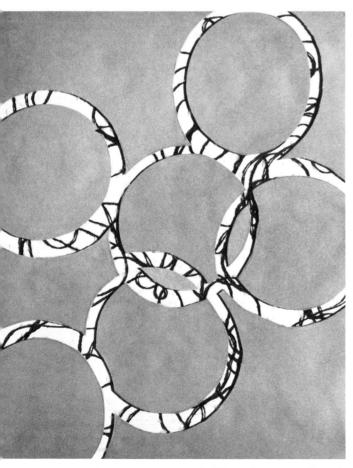

2-15. *Collage*, by Marianita Porterfield; circles in cardboard and string. (Photo by George Suyeoka)

2-17. Collage with dried leaves by Kathleen O'Neal. (Photo by George Suyeoka)

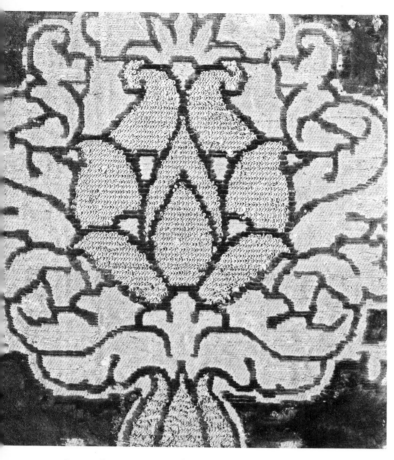

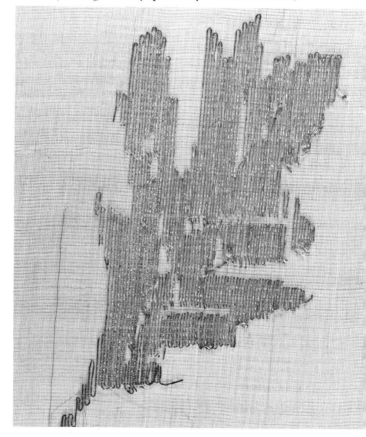

2-18. Flower design (fragment); fifteenth century. (Photo courtesy of The Art Institute of Chicago)

2-20. Panel (part of a dress designed by Jean Worth, 1856-1926). (Photo courtesy of The Art Institute of Chicago)

2-19. Leaf designs (fragment); seventeenth century. (Photo courtesy of The Art Institute of Chicago)

2-21. Brocaded leaf on pima cloth background. (Sample courtesy of Peg Whatley; photo by Bernard Gordon)

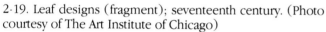

 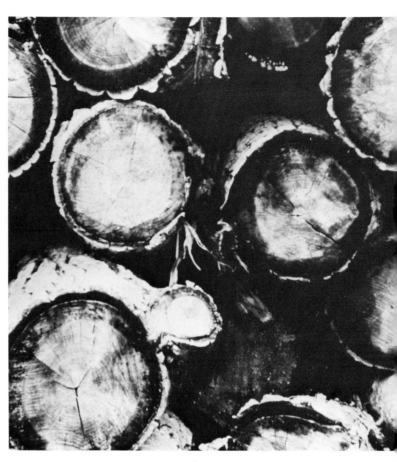

2-22. Leaf design in sixteen-harness twill on painted warp by Irene Wood. (Photo by Bernard Gordon)

2-24. Woodpile in circular design. (Photo courtesy of Dr. Max Kaplan)

2-23. Loom-shaped leaf pile rug by Janet Daniel. (Photo courtesy of Janet Daniel)

2-25. Stone wall in Delphi. (Photo by Else Regensteiner) 2-26. Taliesin wall. (Photo courtesy of James Howlett)

2-27. Gate in Istanbul. (Photo courtesy of Otto E. Nelson)

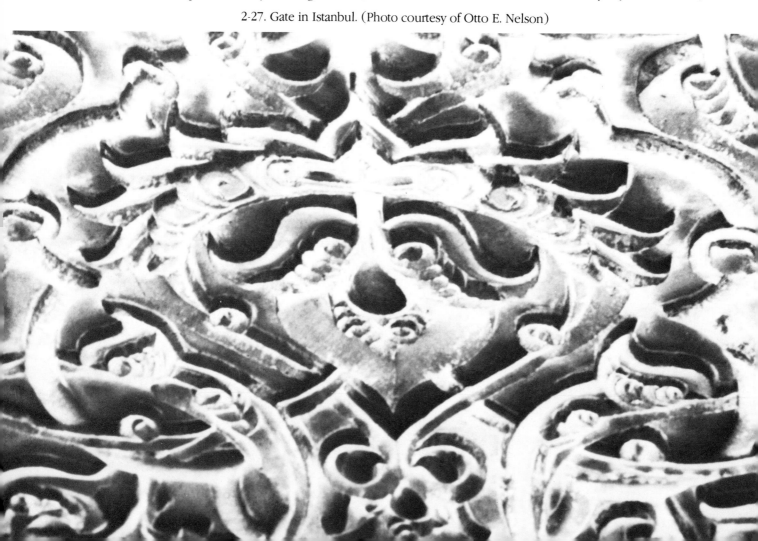

Chapter 3

Designs of Special Significance

Since ancient times the creative spirit, the culture, and the thoughts of mankind have been expressed and preserved in geometric designs. Many of them have become familiar because of their exceptional beauty; others, because of their visual images were transposed into symbolic meanings.

For the weaver, symbols and patterns used in textiles have always been of special interest. Some designs are intricate, stylized interpretations from nature, others change from obvious presentations into expressions of religious beliefs or realistic symbolic art, depicted in the forms of birds, animals, people, or situations. The designs in this chapter have been selected as examples of intriguing and fascinating transformations.

The Paisley Design

The paisley design is associated with the city of Paisley in Scotland but has retained much of the mystery of the Far East, where it originated in a remote region of western India. One of the most frequently used and most beautiful geometric designs, the paisley pattern was derived from a single flower and has evolved into a lovely, distinctive medallion.

The paisley design is used in many forms and many textiles, not only in the famous Kashmir shawls, but also in elaborate variations in Persian rugs and carpets. This design, in more and more intricate variations of twill weaving first devised by expert Persian weavers, was transformed by the Kashmir designers into exquisite shawls of the finest wool spun from the wild Himalayan mountain goat's silky inner fleece, which had to be collected from bushes. As demand for these textiles grew, wool that could be brushed from the fleece of domesticated goats, came into use. These early shawls were handwoven with great skill and were treasured and worn by generations of nobility, including the Mughal Emperor Akbar the Great, who reigned from 1556 to 1605, and his successors, as well as the Empress Josephine of France and Queen Victoria of England in the nineteenth century.

The structure was a combination of tapestry and twill weave, a characteristic of the Kashmir shawls. To ease the strain on the extremely fine warp threads, sett at 80

3-1. Paisley design. (Drawing by Irene Suyeoka)

3-2. Detail of a paisley shawl; twill-tapestry weave. (Collection of Judith Gordon; photo by Bernard Gordon)

3-3. Border of paisley shawl. (Collection of Judith Gordon; photo by Bernard Gordon)

3-4. Geometric paisley design. (Drawing by Irene Suyeoka)

to 100 ends per inch, handlooms were specially adapted with string heddles placed at an even distance from the front beam to the back. The handwoven 2/2 twill tapestry was a reversible fabric, with the changes in color areas made in a double interlocking tapestry technique. This resulted in a ridged joining on the face of the fabric. Geometric transformation of the original flower design was emphasized by the twill weave. Because of the visibility of the warp threads, unusual in traditional tapestry techniques, the twill-tapestry created a nearly iridescent, rather than solid, effect in the shawl cloth.

The dyes used were of subtle and harmonious colors, derived from natural sources: cochineal for red, indigo for blues and purples, saffron for yellows and oranges, and iron filings for black.

The paisley design became so popular in Europe in the early nineteenth century that production of Kashmir-type shawls was adapted first to the drawloom and later to the mechanized Jacquard loom, especially in the city of Paisley. European shawls, woven on drawlooms in France and England, were generally machine woven, while, whether woven or embroidered, the Indian products were made by hand. Quality of texture and design differed greatly in the machine-woven shawls. By the end of the nineteenth century, fashion interest in paisley shawls had subsided.

The many geometric adaptations possible, and evident in, medallions of rugs and patterns of woven and printed

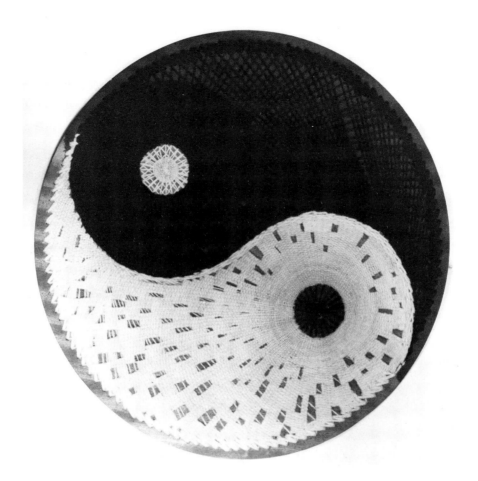

3-5. *Yin Yang,* by Vivienne Mountfort; needle weaving. (Collection of the author; photo by Hector Garcia)

fabrics continue to be a source of inspiration and interest for the contemporary weaver. One example, which is only visually reminiscent of the paisley shape, was made by Vivienne Mountfort, a New Zealand weaver, as a yin-yang design in black and white needle weaving on a wooden disk (fig. 3-5). This Chinese design symbolizes the balance of the masculine and feminine in nature.

Meander, Fret, and Scroll Designs

These designs, developed from the square and diamond shape, have appeared in nearly all cultures of the world.

The meander design's name comes from the Greek word *Maiandros,* which means "winding stream" or "labyrinth". Its path is sharp edged and may turn upon itself in many intricate ways. The meander is sometimes called "Greek key".

The fret design is very similar to the meander. It consists of straight bars intersecting with each other, sometimes in simple, but often in intricate ways. Fret designs are found in many Greek decorations and are also widely used in Far Eastern designs.

The scroll design derives its name from the soft turnings of a paper scroll and has the spiral curves of partly rolled parchment. In nature we frequently find scroll designs in the shells of snails. It appears in many ancient and contemporary textiles.

3-6. Wall of ceremonial building in Mitla, Mexico. (Photo by
Else Regensteiner)

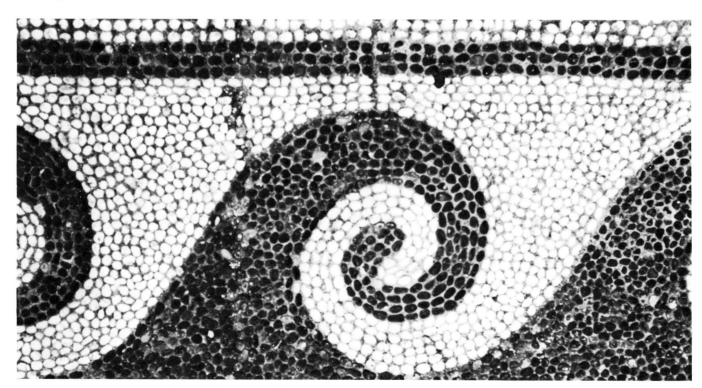

3-7. Pebble mosaic floor with scroll design in Pella, Greece.
(Photo by Else Regensteiner)

3-8. Tail piece (one of a pair) from Peru. (Photo courtesy of The Art Institute of Chicago)

The similarities of these designs in various parts of the world are often striking. Although it is not within the scope of this book to date or trace their origins—a task for archeologists, art historians, and scholars of world history—it is interesting to examine a few examples.

The visitor to Mitla, an archeological site near Oaxaca, Mexico, will find a wall of geometric designs composed of small white stones, fitted together without mortar and set into a background of hard red stucco (fig. 3-6). It is the outer wall of a ceremonial building erected by the Mixtec tribe between 900 and 1300 A.D. In addition to a number of smaller rooms and one larger one, it contained a number of stone shaft tombs. The very stylized designs are thought to be symbols of a feather-serpent deity. This amazing wall clearly shows diamond, meander, scroll, and intricate fret designs.

Meander and fret designs in a variety of complex techniques also appear frequently in textiles of pre-Columbian Peru. The piece shown in figure 3-8 contains as many as seven different techniques, among them tubular plain weave in five colors, looping, oblique twill interlacing, complementary warp, dove-tailing, and braiding. Another fragment (fig. 3-9) from the north coast of Peru shows variations of the fret design carried out within the same piece in plain weave, discontinuous wefts, and dove-tailing tapestry methods.

3-9. Fragment; Peru, north coast, Mochica style. (Photo courtesy of The Art Institute of Chicago)

3-12. Meander or fret design in color-and-weave effect by Judith Gordon. (Photo courtesy of Judith Gordon)

The meander design woven fringe shown in figure 3-10, a rug border from Ambato, Ecuador, in figure 3-11, and the contemporary interpretations in figures 3-12 through 3-16 all illustrate the diversity of these attractive patterns. (Note that the meander design in figure 3-13 was woven on a 16-harness loom in Beiderwand technique. This weaving structure is explained on pages 67 to 89 of *Weaving Sourcebook*. References for weaving the fabrics in figures 3-14 and 3-15 may be found on page 66 of *The Art of Weaving*, Third Edition).

3-10. Woven fringe from Peru in slit tapestry technique. (Collection of the author; Photo by Hector Garcia)

3-11. Border of pile rug from Ambato, Ecuador. (Photo by Else Regensteiner)

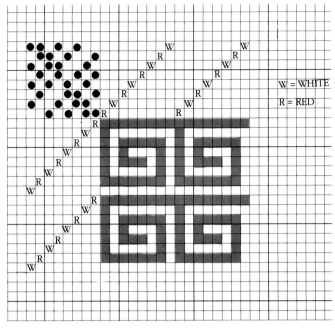

W = WHITE
R = RED

3-12a. Draft and diagram for figure 3-12.

3-15. Detail of figure 3-14.

3-14. Meander design in double weave by Takeko Nomiya. (Photo by Edward Miller)

3-13. Meander variation by Judith Gordon. (Photo by Bernard Gordon)

3-16. Pyramid structure by Irene Suyeoka. (Photo by George Suyeoka)

3-17. Chilkat-style. Blanket, Tlingit tribe, northwest coast, British Columbia. (Photo courtesy of The Art Institute of Chicago)

The Chilkat Blanket

Geometric designs of symbolic meaning can be found in the ceremonial shoulder capes and dancing blankets of the Tlingit Indians, who lived first on the northwest coast between British Columbia and the United States and later settled on the coast of southeastern Alaska, where the first European contact was made in the late eighteenth century. The Chilkats, a tribe of the Tlingit Indians, adopted their name from the river that cut its way from the interior mountains to the sea. Ceremonial blankets collected during the first third of the nineteenth century were already heirlooms of the tribe. Some Chilkat blankets are beautifully preserved and can be seen in museums of Europe and the Americas.

The blankets typically have a horizontal top and a curved lower border with fringes (fig. 3-17). The surface is divided into various geometric units. Symbolic designs usually represent an animal of special significance, such as the raven, beaver, bear, wolf, or hawk. Various design units represent the head, the body, the tail, the hips, and the joints of the animal, depending on their placement within the blanket. Most striking is the use of an oval or round field, the ever present eye design. The blankets were always designed by the men of the tribe, who painted half of the design on a wooden board. The women completed the design in the weaving.

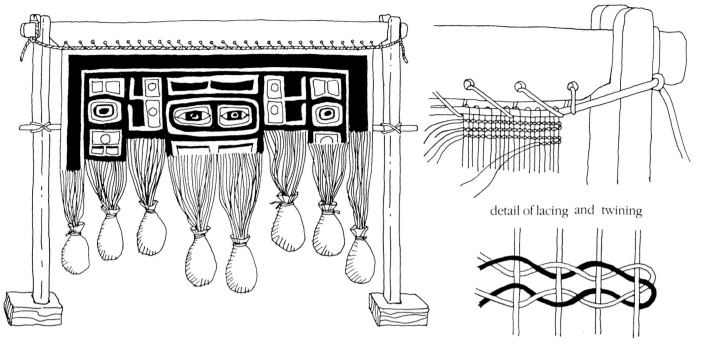

detail of lacing and twining

detail of twining when turning corners

3-18. Chilkat blanket on loom (Drawings by George Suyeoka)

The Chilkat loom, of which an excellent example is shown in "Maritime Peoples of the Arctic and Northwest Coast", a permanent exhibition at the Field Museum of Natural History in Chicago, consists of two upright beams supported by blocks of wood at the base, a wooden crossbeam at the top, and a wooden bar at the upper third of the weaving space. Holes were drilled into the top beam at even distances. A rope for holding the warp was tied to the top posts and held in place by a string lashed through the holes. The warp was strung over this rope in pairs and held apart by several rows of twining (fig. 3-18). Since the technique of construction was twining, no rigid tension was required. The free-hanging warp was gathered in bundles into gut bags and stretched by its own weight.

The warps of the Chilkat blankets were made from the inner bark of the cedar tree, coated with wool of the mountain goat and spun first with an S-twist and then plied tightly with two strands in Z-twist direction. The weft consisted of two-strand goat wool in white and natural shades, accented by black, yellow, and pale green areas dyed from natural plant material.

Twining of the intricate curves and angles of the outlines required several ingenious techniques, which are illustrated in figure 3-19. Divisons were joined by a fine sinew cord, and an overlay of three-strand plaiting hid any irregularities caused by manipulation of the shapes.

The contemporary weaver can find much inspiration not only in the unique geometric shapes, but also in the application of a technique that appears anything but primitive when seen in the superior craftsmanship of the Tlingit Indians.

3-19. Various twining techniques used in Chilkat blankets (Drawings by George Suyeoka)

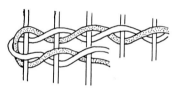

two-color twining showing turns over and under one warp thread

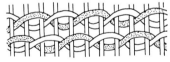

Two-color twining over and under two warp threads, with alternate colors entwining alternate pairs of warp threads to create a twill effect

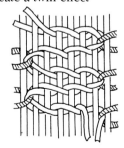

interlocked two-strand twining

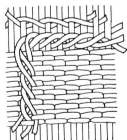

three-strand twining used to outline motifs

three-thread weft twining

4-1. Greek Parthenon. (Photo by Else Regensteiner)

Chapter 4

Systems of Design

Ratios and Dynamic Symmetry

The beauty of a work of art is based on a sense of perfection that appeals, consciously or unconsciously, to the sensitivity of the viewer or user. A true work of art, whether a painting or sculpture, a textile or a building, never loses its harmony and balance with the passage of time. In analyzing the intrinsic qualities of such a work, we soon realize that the secret of its eternal value lies in its proportions and the relationships of its parts to one another.

The ancient architects and master builders were the first to use specific geometrical proportions to produce the greatest examples of Greek art. An early statement of this aesthetic order can be found in *De Divina Proportione*, written by Fra Luca Pacioli in 1509. These proportions later became known as "The Golden Section", "The Golden Rule", or "The Golden Mean". The scientist Johann Kepler called them a "precious jewel". The ancient Greeks defined the *Golden Mean* as the point that divides a line in such a manner that the smaller part is in the same proportion to the larger part as the larger part is to the entire line. The ratio determined to be the ideal relationship of space division was the proportion of 1 to 1.618, or an approximate simplified proportion of 5 to 8. The Parthenon in Athens, Greece (fig. 4-1) is a perfect example of this theory.

In 1202, a mathematician from Pisa published a study of progressive numbers known as the *Fibonacci series*. It is said that through a study of the propagation rate of a pair of hypothetical rabbits, Leonardo Fibonacci established a relationship of numbers in nature that correspond, after the fourteenth number in the series, to the ratio of the Golden Rule. Starting with 1,1, each progressive number in the series is the sum of the two previous numbers. Therefore the progression of numbers is 1, 2, 3, 5, 8, 13, 21, 34, and so on, continued indefinitely. This constant ratio is found in ancient as well as contemporary design proportions, from the Greek Parthenon to modern architecture, from great paintings to commercial shapes of rugs, windows, and doors. It is also the proportion in all nature and is found in the distribution of seeds and petals of flowers, in the progression of spirals in shells and snails, in the arrangements of leaves and branches on a stem, and, most strikingly, in the division of the human body. Any numbers in the series will work together and can be used as a guide for proportions in measurements of inches, for space divisions, for the number of threads in a border, and for distribution of shapes. The result is always pleasing.

Jay Hambidge, whose book *Elements of Dynamic Symmetry* was first published in 1920, has spent years studying Greek art and architecture, seeking to derive empirical design principles to support his theory that great art of the past did not derive so much from instinctive art ability as from a standardized body of design principles with considerable scientific base. Analyzing art forms and architectural shapes, Hambidge noted that as the length of rectangles (with similar heights) increased, the increments were proportional increases corresponding to the symmetrical growth patterns found in man and nature. Arriving at conclusions such as Fibonacci had drawn in his series of numbers, Hambidge then applied them to graphic divisions of space. Two design principles are distinguished: static and dynamic symmetry. *Static symmetry* has a fixed entity or state. It is rigid in the orderly arrangement of units around a center and appears in nature most obviously in the structure of infinite varieties of snowflakes (fig. 4-5). *Dynamic symmetry*, as found in all

4-2. Scroll design from Ephesus, Greece. (Photo by Else Regensteiner)

4-3. Tree and its shadow, Guatemala.

4-4. Sunflower head. (Drawing by Irene Suyeoka)

growth of plants and shells, is moving and flowing (fig.4-6)

Reduced from complex mathematics to simplified explanations, the principles of dynamic symmetry can be presented in a concrete way in a series of root rectangles. Exercises by which dimensions of dynamic symmetry can be established help the weaver to find excellent divisions of space for many projects. Once the perimeter of a piece, planned by the weaver, is established, the space within can be subdivided by constructing appropriate diagonals, horizontals, verticals, and curves according to the dynamic symmetry system. These spaces can then be used for the placement of motifs, colors, and textures for a successful design.

The square root of a quantity is a number that, when multiplied by itself gives that quantity. The square root of 16 is 4 because 4 x 4 is 16. Or the square root of 25 is 5 because 5 x 5 equals 25. When the square root of a number is graphically expressed in exact parts of one, a perfect square is root one. From this square other units are developed, as shown in figures 4-7 to 4-10.

Constructing Divisions of Space

Constructing divisions of space based on dynamic symmetry must be done with a compass. This simple instrument for describing circles or transferring measurements consists of two pointed branches (one of them holding a pencil), joined at the top by a pivot. I am greatly indebted to Sadye Tune Wilson who compiled and clarified the diagrams illustrating the ways by which a weaver can divide space into pleasing and "just right" proportions (fig. 4-7, 4-8, 4-9). Her drawings explain step by step how rectangles can be constructed with the help of the compass and how pleasing divisions of space are made with the additions of diagonal, vertical, and horizontal lines.

Start with the basic unit of root one, the square, and draw a diagonal line through it from corner to corner. With the compass, measure the length of that diagonal and draw a curve with this length from the lower left-hand corner of the square. This adds an extension to the original base line of the square. When the horizontal and vertical lines are drawn in, a root 2 rectangle is established.

Once this first step is understood and practiced a few times, the next steps, which establish progressively larger dimensions are easy. The mathematical numbers become the proportions of dynamic symmetry. I urge the weaver to draw the diagrams from the root 2 rectangle through the root 5 rectangle in the way they are presented. Further steps demonstrate how to construct rectangles from the diagonal of half a square and how to arrive at the classical proportion of the "Golden Mean" by constructing what Hambidge called the "Whirling Square Rectangle". With subdivisions, intricate and exciting designs made in this way can serve as points of departure for the weaving of beautiful textiles.

4-5. Snowflakes. (Drawing by George Suyeoka)

4-6. Growth of spiral in a shell. (Drawing by George Suyeoka)

Rectangles Constructed from the Diagonal of a Square

1. The basic unit is the square, which can be any desired size. From this basic unit (root 1), a rectangle is constructed by drawing a diagonal from one corner to the other (fig 4-7A).

2. This diagonal of the root 1 rectangle becomes the base of the root 2 rectangle. The compass, using the length of the diagonal as measurement, extends the baseline out to establish the size of the root 2 rectangle (fig. 4-7B). The extended space is 0.414. The area of this rectangle is therefore 1 (the square) + 0.414 or √2 = 1.414.

3. The diagonal of the root 2 rectangle becomes the base of the root 3 rectangle (fig. 4-7C). The extended space is 0.7 32. The area of this rectangle is therefore 1 (the square) + 0.732 or √3 = 1.732.

4. The area of root 4 rectangle (√4= 2.000) is two square units (fig. 4.7D).

5. The diagonal of the root 4 rectangle establishes the base of the root 5 rectangle (fig. 4-7E). This area is two square units + 0.236 or √5 = 2.236.

6. The diagonal of the root 5 rectangle becomes the base of the root 6 rectangle and so on. However, root rectangles higher than root 5 are rarely used, although combinations of the basic rectangular shapes are utilized. A wide variety of space divisions can accommodate any number of designs.

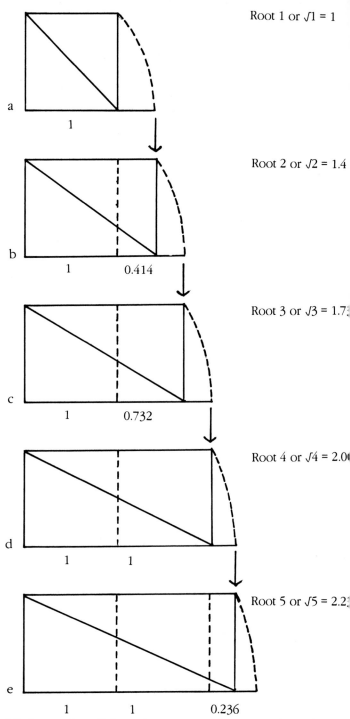

Root 1 or √1 = 1

Root 2 or √2 = 1.4

Root 3 or √3 = 1.7

Root 4 or √4 = 2.00

Root 5 or √5 = 2.2

4-7. Rectangles of dynamic symmetry. (Diagrams by Sadye Tune Wilson)

Rectangles Constructed from the Diagonal of Half a Square

The diagonal constructed from half a square adds a dimension of 0.618 to the square. This converts the rectangle into an area of 1.618, which Jay Hambidge named a *Whirling Square* (fig. 4-8). It is also the *Golden Section* of classical proportions. By adding a 0.618 rectangle to the opposite end of the whirling square rectangle, the rectangle becomes a root 5 rectangle (0.618 + 1 + 0.618 = 2.236). The 0.618 section is itself a whirling square rectangle. The root 5 rectangle and its *Golden Section* were used extensively in Greek art and architecture. The relationships within and among the rectangles become an intriguing study for the designer (fig. 4-9).

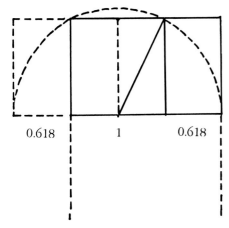

construction of the Whirling Square rectangle

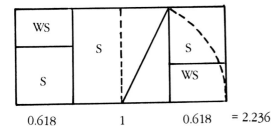

b

root 5 rectangle with basic shapes subdividing the whole rectangle constructed from the diagonal of *half* a square

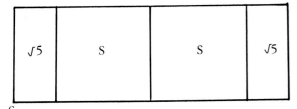

c

compound rectangle composed of basic shapes forming a whole

4-8. Whirling Square—The Golden Section of the root 5 rectangle

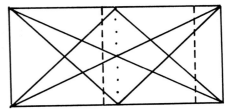

a

Vertical at intersection of diagonal with perimeter

b

Vertical at intersection of diagonals

4-9. a. root 5 rectangle with subdivisions; b. two Whirling Square rectangles subdivided.

Design Approaches: A Basic Rectangle As a Design Unit

In any design unit—square, root rectangle, or whirling square rectangle—variety can be introduced through the construction of diagonals, horizontals, and verticals within the linear bounds in order to produce rhythmic themes. Logical subdivisions are made by using diagonals of the square and of the root rectangles and by constructing horizontals and verticals at the point of intersection of the diagonals or at the point of intersection of a diagonal with the perimeters of the shape.

Compound Rectangle

A unit square, root rectangle, or whirling square rectangle may be used in combination with itself or with other units as multiples or additives to produce a compound rectangle. Variety within the compound rectangle can be introduced through the construction of diagonals, horizontals, and verticals within the linear bounds of the compound rectangle, as well as within the linear bounds of basic rectangles or squares (fig. 4-10).

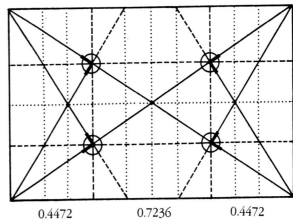

4-10a. Dynamic symmetry; divisions constructed from points where diagonals cross. (Diagram by George McVicker)

A weaving design based on objective rules of symmetry is well on the way to becoming a good design. Exploring and experimenting with those rules offers many rewarding possibilities. They are a great help and challenge to the weaver but should never limit the creative approach. The choice of colors, textures, materials, and weave structures, applied to true and proven dimensions, will do their share to assure a personal expression and creative statement in every woven work of art.

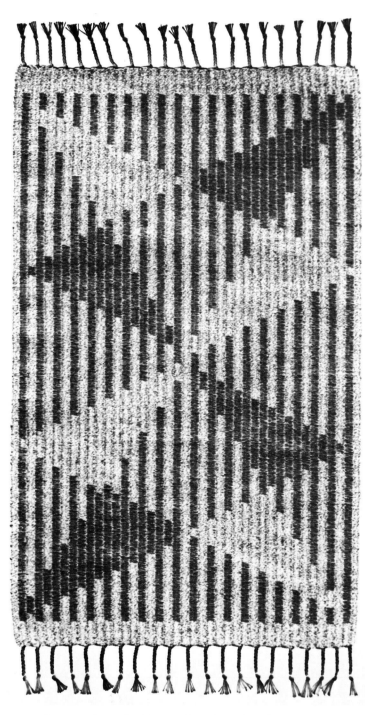

4-10. Rug by Sadye Tune Wilson, based on dynamic symmetry divisions of space. (Photo courtesy of Sadye Tune Wilson)

Tessellation

The term *Tessellation* is derived from the Latin word "tessellare", to pave with tiles. Webster's definition is "a careful juxtaposition of elements into a coherent pattern". Weavers are familiar with mosaics in floor tiles, tiles for decoration, and quilt patterns derived from ancient designs. A characteristic of most tile design is repetition. A line figure may be used repetitively to cover a surface, or a given design motif may be used as the repeat element. Only three figures—squares, triangles, and hexagons—will combine in an allover pattern; intervals occur when combining other regular figures, octagons, or pentagons, for example. Contemporary books such as *Geometry of Art and Life* by Matila Ghyka or ancient works such as *The Thirteen Books of Euclid's Elements, The Works of Archimedes,* and *Conics of Apollonius* give mathematical explanations and many figures that suggest tessellation designs in never ending variations.

Experimenting with tessellation designs can be easy and enjoyable. Use cut paper or pencil sketches and place small shapes on a contrasting background. As

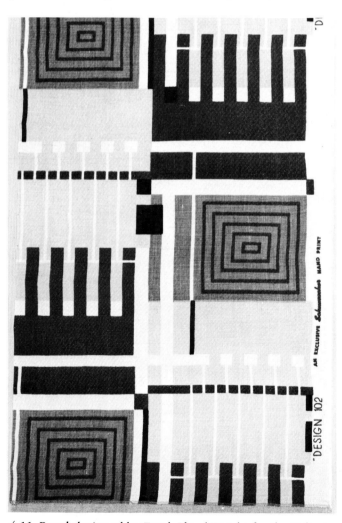

4-11. Panel designed by Frank Lloyd Wright for the Taliesin line of decorative fabrics and wallpapers. (Photo courtesy of The Art Institute of Chicago)

interesting designs or motifs occur, place one or several small hand mirrors next to or around the design to see the repetition of the patterns. Kaleidoscopic pattern changes may be seen by slowly moving the mirrors left, right, up, down, or diagonally over the design surface. Additional pattern changes are achieved by holding the mirrors at various angles to each other as they move over the design. *Tessellation Design with Three Mirrors* (fig. 4-13) demonstrates the many magical results performed with mirrors. Figures 4-14 through 4-19 show basic tessellation line elements.

4-12. *Zèbres,* hanging in cotton and wool tapestry weave; executed at the Atelier Tabard Frères et Soeurs, Aubusson, France; cartoon by Victor Vasarely. (Photo courtesy of The Art Institute of Chicago)

4-13. *Tessellation Design with Three Mirrors,* by Sadye Tune Wilson. (Photo courtesy of Sadye Tune Wilson)

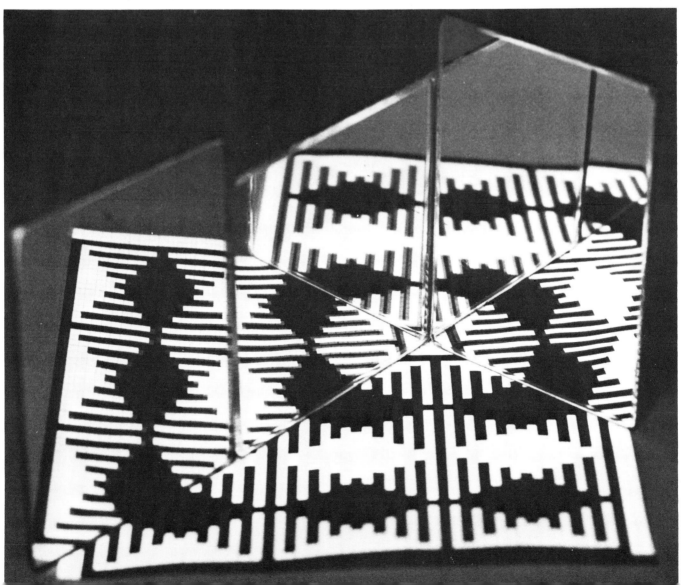

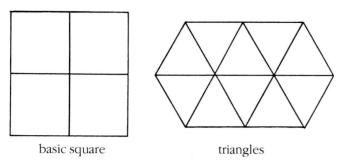

basic square   triangles

4-14. Tessellation (Diagrams by Sadye Tune Wilson)

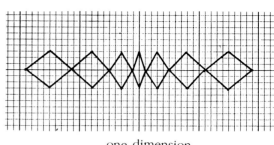

one dimension

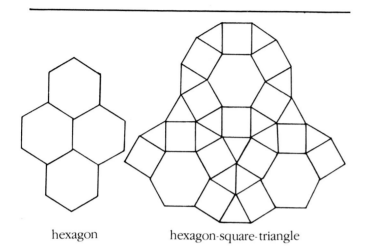

hexagon   hexagon-square-triangle

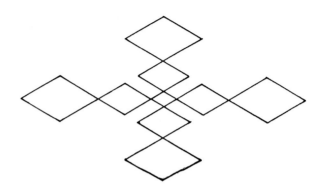

two dimensions, especially useful in designing radiating patterns

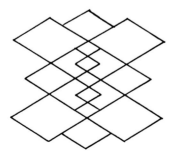

hexagon-triangle   square-triangle

4-15. Plane partitions combined in all-over design

4-17. Graduate size of pattern in one or two dimensions progressively. Eliminate lines to create new elements.

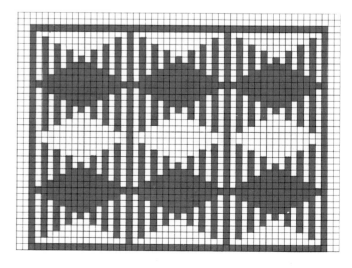

4-16. Tessellation design modifications: expand or contract the design element.

4-18. Use color or shading to create shapes within shapes.

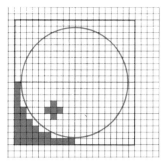

motif based on circle inscribed
in square

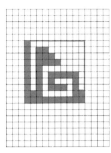

motif based on square circumscribing
design element

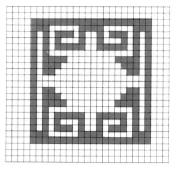

rotation of design element
to create pattern

4-19. Plane partitions inscribing and circumscribing design element

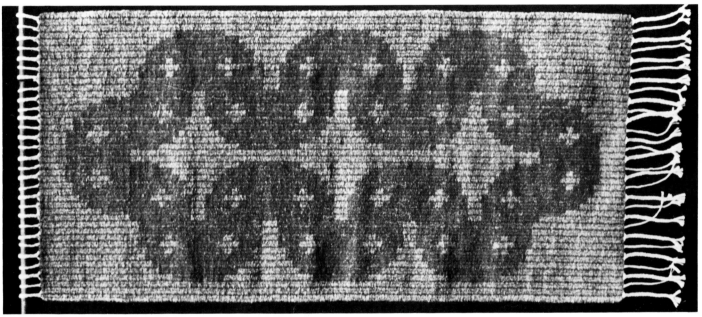

4-20. Rug in tessellation pattern by Sadye Tune Wilson.
Rotation of the design element is used to create pattern in a
motif based on a circle inscribed in a square. (Collection of
Dr. and Mrs. Carl Kuttruff; photo courtesy of Sadye Tune
Wilson)

4-20a. Diagrams for figure 4-20.

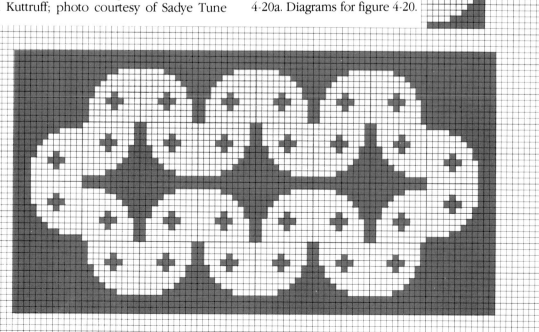

4-22. Rug in Karakul and Icelandic wool by Jane Busse. (Photo courtesy of Jane Busse)

4-21. *Ekinrode,* by Merle Hillary Shusner. Tessellation design in interlocking tapestry technique. (Photo by John Herr courtesy of Merle Hillary Shusner)

4-23. Modular design. (Diagram by Anna Day)

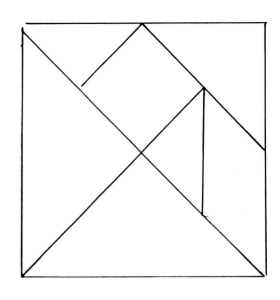

4-24. Seven divisions of space in a Chinese tangram toy.

4-25. Modular design with four units in double weave by Irene Suyeoka. (Photo by George Suyeoka)

The Module

Modular units are well known in many fields of art, architecture, and design. Furniture manufacturers offer modular units for combinations of shelves, cabinets, and desks. Le Corbusier, the modern architect, became famous for establishing the module as a valid form of composition. Children play with modules of flat pieces of cardboard or plastics that fit together for creative designs and shapes.

The module, as defined by Webster, is "a standard unit of measurement". Units of a size and shape with common measurements will fit together to fill a given space and can be arranged and rearranged in many different ways. The weaver, too, can use modules to express decorative design ideas. They are often separate pieces, which can be arranged in any number of combinations.

Ken Weaver composed multiple panels of bright rep weaves and three sections of *Cone Forms* in woven, sewn, and shaped units for a commissioned wall piece of strong geometric design (fig. 4-26). Characteristic of rep weaves are ridges made by alternating heavy and thin yarns. His units consist of tightly woven warp-faced rep strips with warps of 36 to 42 ends per inch, crossed with wefts of 30 to 40 ends of two-ply wool wound together for the large pick and one end of 20/2 linen in between for the thin pick. The strips are cut into small pieces, which are machine sewn into "cones"; these are then sewn together for the final hanging.

Janet Daniel's *Cascade* shows single units with variations, including size, shape, and texture (fig. 4-28). The three panels of modules shown in figure 4-29 are based on diamond shapes and triangles.

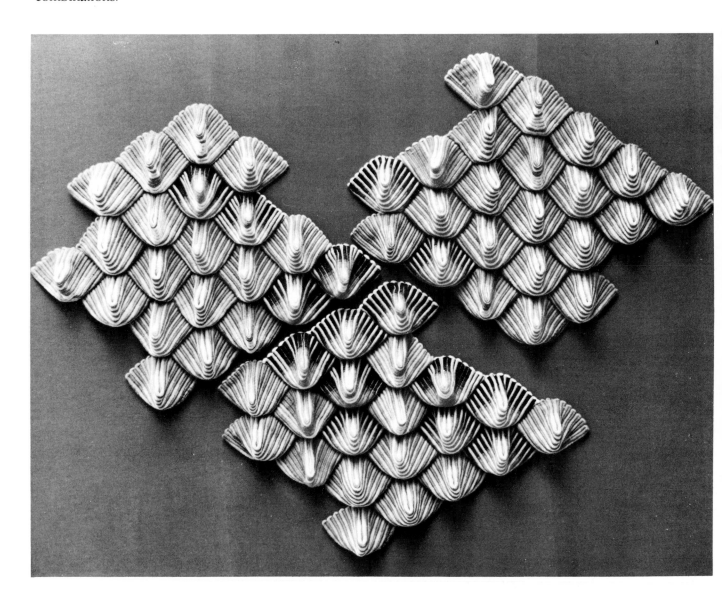

4-26. *Cone Forms,* by Ken Weaver; modular wall piece in three sections based on the diamond shape. (Photo courtesy of Ken Weaver)

4-27. Multiple panel rep weave by Ken Weaver; colors include bright reds, oranges, yellows, wines, purples, and hot pinks. (Photo courtesy of Ken Weaver)

4-28. *Cascade,* by Janet Daniel; wall hanging in seven separate pieces. (Photo courtesy of Janet Daniel)

4-29. Modular units designed by Philip E. Smith and woven at the American Farm School in Thessaloniki, Greece. (Photo by Else Regensteiner)

61

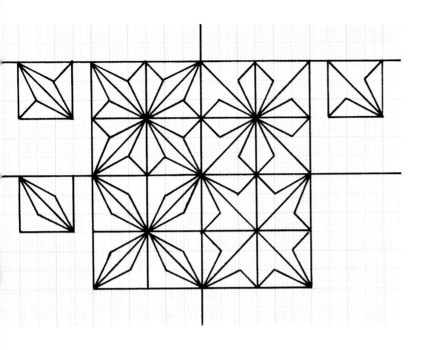

4-30. Design on grid by Sadye Tune Wilson; the elimination of lines creates new elements.

4-31. *Chicago Checkerboard,* by Anne Wilson; wall hanging in linen, rayon, abaca. (Photo by Dean Jacobson; courtesy of Anne Wilson)

4-32. Detail of *Chicago Checkerboard,* by Anne Wilson. (Photo by Dean Jacobson, courtesy of Anne Wilson)

The Grid

Weavers use the grid for drafting patterns and plotting designs. It is a network of uniformly spaced horizontal and perpendicular lines and is used extensively by artists for scaling geometric shapes and proportions. Classic architects used the grid to compose perspective and size relationships, and graphic designers ancient and modern, used it to design letters and the layout of the printed page.

The grid can be visible or invisible in the final design. It can be simple or complex and can have regular spaces of squares, rectangles, hexagons, diamonds, and free divisions, but its main characteristic is the regularity with which a surface is covered. Although the grid is usually used simply as a design guide, some artists have made it an integral part of their designs. One such person is artist-weaver Anne Wilson, who uses the visible grid extensively in its most basic form, the square, giving it life and substance through imaginative selection of materials and textures (fig. 4-32). The static background, in contrast with the fluid and lively surface, gives Wilson's weavings a thoroughly satisfying unity.

The grid can be used in plain weaves, double weaves, and tapestry techniques. The Navajo blanket shown in figure 4-36 uses squares and rectangular grid background, and includes geometric designs in unusually exciting combinations.

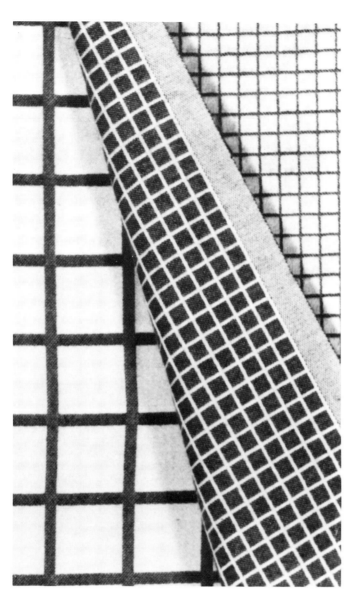

4-33. *Check and Double Check,* from the Graphics Collection by Jack Lenor Larsen. (Photo courtesy of Jack Lenor Larsen, Inc)

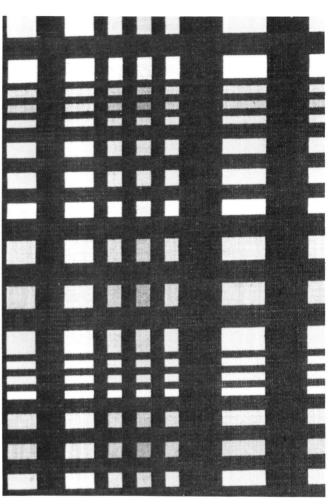

4-34. *Moire Stripes,* the Graphics Collection by Jack Lenor Larsen. (Photo courtesy of Jack Lenor Larsen, Inc)

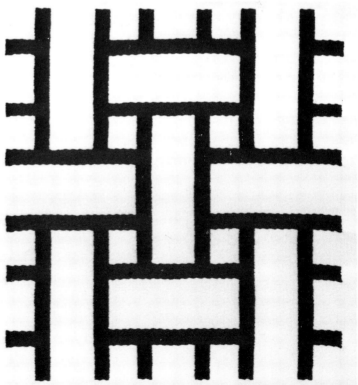

4-35. Tapestry design in black and white wool by Marie Eckl. (Photo courtesy of Marie Eckl)

63

4-36. Navajo blanket; geometric shapes on grid divisions. (Courtesy of the Denver Art Museum, Denver, Colorado)

5-1. Antique Oushak garden carpet; Turkish, mid-nineteenth century (Photo by Otto E. Nelson; courtesy of Vojtech Blau Inc.)

Part II
Weaver-Controlled Techniques

5-2. Antique Heriz rug. (Photo by Otto E. Nelson; courtesy of
Vojtech Blau Inc.)

Chapter 5

Designs in Rug Techniques

In weaving we distinguish among textiles that are made by hand, textiles whose patterns are controlled entirely by the action of the loom, and fabrics that are mechanically produced by the power loom. As hand-weavers we are concerned with the first two methods, although any of the designs made by hand can be used as prototypes for production by industry.

When a design is executed freely by the weaver's hand and therefore under his or her spontaneous control, the method is classified as *weaver-controlled*. Usually the handloom is the implement on which the work is done. Of the weaver-controlled techniques, the knotted rug, the wrapping methods as seen in the Soumak, the tapestry techniques, and the laid-in and pick-up methods, including pick-up double weave, lend themselves most successfully to planning and executing geometric designs.

One of the most important projects a weaver can plan is the production of a handwoven rug. The method of knotting and wrapping cannot be reproduced by machine and weavers who use the ancient methods to weave rugs in pile and tapestry techniques in new and contemporary designs will find inspiration and incentive in the beauty of fine oriental rugs.

Oriental Pile Rugs

Many fine oriental rugs have been handed down as heirlooms from generation to generation, and they are useful and lasting additions to home and life.

Persia (the present-day Iran), Turkey and the Caucasus, Turkestan and Afghanistan, Pakistan, India, and China all have produced rugs with distinctive features, known and treasured for many centuries.

Western weavers should not try to copy the traditional oriental rug. Its beauty depends on distinctive designs, traditional craftsmanship, very dense knotting, masterly attention to detail, and a specific palette of colors all of which, together with intricate distribution of patterns, have a distinct definite style that would become stale and false with such attempts.

A study of geometric designs must, however, include oriental pile rugs: their huge variety of two-dimensional shapes, their overall composition, their masterly hand-

ling of relationships of one shape to another and the whole rug, and, last but not least, the rich blending of colors, which glow when new and mellow with age. These jewels of the carpet maker's art can be true inspirations for geometric designs, their distribution and composition, and can be absorbed and translated for the weaver's own creative growth.

5-3. Antique Bakshaish rug; northwest Persian, mid-nineteenth century. (Photo by Otto E. Nelson; courtesy of Vojtech Blau Inc.)

Many symbolic meanings were originally attached to the designs, of which the prayer rug is an important example (fig. 5-4). A niche, called "mihrab", on which the faithful kneel to pray, is outlined as a distinctive arch, with its point directed toward Mecca. The niche is supposed to represent the alcove in the great mosque of Mecca. Symbolic significance was also given to stylized flowers, plants, animals, birds, and fruit. Such familiar symbols as the pear or pine-cone design, known as "boteh" and much later as paisley, and the "Tree of Life" have worked their way into many cultures.

Some colors, too, have symbolic meanings: Red is joy, life, good virtues; white, a symbol of mourning; purple is an imperial color; moghul blue and yellow are Chinese royal colors; and rose signifies divine wisdom.

Stylized creatures also appear as symbols: The scorpion and tarantula are rightly symbols of viciousness and poison, while the camel represents wealth and happiness. Geometrics such as diamonds, octagons, stars, and crosses, appear in untold combinations and variations. In former times, an oriental rug's origin could be determined by its distinctive designs, but today the same or similar designs are executed in rugs of many districts or even countries and are woven strictly as decorative art. Nevertheless, Charles Jacobsen, in his book *Oriental Rugs*, is right when he states: "No two similar designs in the same rug are exactly alike. It is the many little differences and changes that makes the Oriental Rug so interesting and beautiful".

One of the most subtle characteristics of Persian rug design is the fine, often almost imperceptible outline in different colors, which provides a boundary to each individual design. The field of color appears to be different every time, depending on the influence of this boundary edge. Weavers familiar with the color studies of Joseph Albers and Johannes Itten (see Bibliography) can easily recognize, apply, and understand these important changes.

Production

Oriental rugs are always hand-made, and the knots can be seen on the reverse side. Machine-made imitations are easily discernible by the lack of these knots at the back of the rug. There are still weavers who are thoroughly familiar with traditional patterns and produce rugs, one at a time, on an individual basis. In

5-4. Prayer rug. (Drawing by Irene Suyeoka)

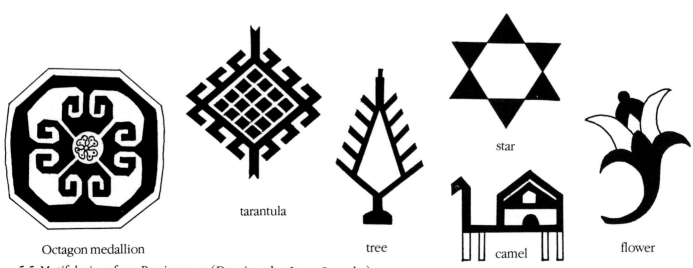

tarantula

Octagon medallion

tree

star

camel

flower

5-5. Motif designs from Persian rugs (Drawings by Irene Suyeoka)

5-6. Detail of oriental geometric pile rug. (Collection of the author; photo by Hector Garcia)

some cases, scale models drawn on small-square graph paper are used, with each square defining one knot or one color area. In so-called rug factories, several rugs of the same design are woven simultaneously, with a master weaver or "Mirzah" calling or chanting off the colors of the knots to the weavers, who complete row after row, with one to three tabby shots in between. On large carpets, several weavers work side by side.

Looms

Looms used by nomadic tribes for rug making have to be portable; they produce only narrow widths. These looms consist of two poles around which the warp threads are tied. To stretch the warp, in this case in a horizontal direction, stakes are driven into the ground. When the tribe moves on, the loom is simply rolled up without detaching the rug so that work on it can be resumed later.

Upright looms can be of several types. The village type consists of a fixed horizontal beam and a lower, or cloth, beam, the ends of which fit into the slots of two vertical beams. The weavers sit on a plank resting on the bottom rung of two ladders. As the work progresses, the plank is raised.

5-7. Stylized flower from center of Persian carpet. (Collection of the author; photo by Hector Garcia)

5-8. Village rug weavers in Turkey. (Photo by Else Regensteiner)

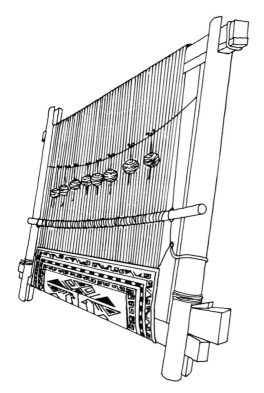

5-9. Oriental rug loom, Tabriz type. (Drawing by George Suyeoka)

The Tabriz-type loom (fig.5-9) and the roller beam loom are usually used to weave carpets that are at least twice the length of the upright beams. In the first type, the warp is wound in a continuous length around the top and bottom beams and therefore can be moved by loosening the holding wedges. The warp is pulled down as the weaving proceeds, and the weavers do not have to change their position.

The roller-type looms can carry carpets of any length. A simple mechanism is used to separate the warp threads into two sheds through which the wefts pass after each row of knots. Balls of colored wool for the pile are hung across the loom at a convenient height.

Material

The principal material in all oriental rugs is sheep wool. Camel hair, silk, or goat wool is used in rare cases. Warp and tabby in Persian rugs are usually cotton, superior to wool for wear and quality. The beautiful wool pile is the dominant feature; the warp and weft picks are the sturdy but invisible background.

Knots

Two principal knots are used to make oriental pile rugs: the Ghiordes or Turkish knot and the Sehna or Persian knot (fig. 5-10). The density of the pile is a very important factor. In a good oriental rug, there are as many as 300 to 800 knots in one square inch, with an experienced craftsman knotting as many as 8,000 knots per day. From one to three picks are thrown across in a plain weave shed after each row of knots. If three picks are used, two are stretched tight, while the center one is left sinuous. The weft is beaten down with a wooden comb.

Wooden comb used by Oriental rug weavers

Ghiordes or Turkish knot   Sehna or Persian knot

5-10. (drawing by George Suyeoka)

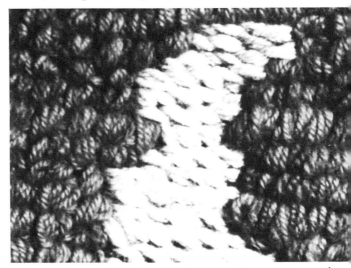

5-11. *Phoenix,* (detail) by Martha Dean; wall piece in Soumak technique. From the collection of Dr. Ruby L. Koschene. (Photo courtesy of Martha Dean)

Soumak Rugs

Strong geometric patterns are found in the rare old rugs worked in a flat knotted technique named after the place of their origin, Shemakha or Soumak, near the Caspian Sea in the Caucasus. Rectangles, octagons, stars, and bands are characteristic of these rugs. The technique is wrapping, rather than knotting, and gives a flat but raised surface similar to that of embroidery. Contemporary weavers frequently use this technique to give textured accents to flat-woven textiles.

The weft is wool, used in a closed shed on a cotton, wool or linen warp. The weft can travel over one, two, or more warp threads, resulting in a finer or coarser surface. One tabby is thrown in alternating sheds after each row of wrapping is completed. The slant depends on whether wrapping starts from the right or the left side of the warp. When the weft travels first from left to right and returns after the tabby pick from right to left, an effect similar to chain-stitch is the result.

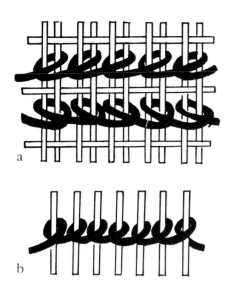

5-12. a. Soumak wrapping over two warp threads; b. Soumak wrapping over one warp thread.

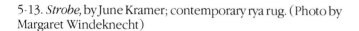

5-13. *Strobe,* by June Kramer; contemporary rya rug. (Photo by Margaret Windeknecht)

Rya and Flossa Rugs

The same Ghiordes knot found in oriental carpets is used to make the subtle and richly textured Scandinavian rugs known as rya and flossa. Their geometric designs are simpler and less crowded than those of oriental rugs, but the influence of ornamentation is obvious in the diamond, stripe, checkerboard, triangle, star, and cross designs used.

These rugs were originally used as coverlets; the knotted pile faced downward while the background was the surface. Today, rya and flossa rugs are used as floor coverings or wall hangings and have a principally decorative function.

The surface of the rya is quite shaggy because the knotted pile is longer and more tabby picks keep the knotted rows farther apart. The threads of the pile must be long enough to cover six to ten rows of plain weave and therefore have a tendency to lie flat. This makes the outlines of designs softer and often blurred.

In the flossa rug, the pile is also knotted in the Ghiordes knot technique, but it is shorter and more dense because fewer tabby picks are placed between the knotted rows. As a result, the pile stands up straight after a few rows have been completed. Designs are isolated and outlines defined clearly.

A third version is called half-flossa: only the pattern is woven in pile; the flat ground, however, also forms part of the design.

5-14. Rya carpet from central Finland, early eighteenth century. (Photo courtesy of The Art Institute of Chicago)

Material

As in oriental rugs, the best yarn for rya and flossa pile is wool, but contemporary weavers have also successfully used mohair, linen, or hemp for interesting variations. Several strands of yarns should be used in each knot, with subtle color blending, to add beauty and depth to the pile.

The warp is cotton or linen and, depending on the desired density, the length of the pile, and the number of tabby picks planned, sett at 6 to 10 ends per inch. Tabbies must cover the warp completely in order to produce a firm and flat background. As in all functional textiles, wearing quality is an important consideration, and beautiful rugs, comparable to museum pieces, can be woven today as heirlooms for tomorrow.

5-15. Contemporary hanging in combination of pile, weft floats, tapestry, and plain weave areas; Stockholm, Sweden, twentieth century. (Photo courtesy of The Art Institute of Chicago)

Combinations of Techniques

In oriental rugs, variations in height are sometimes achieved by "sculpturing" the dense pile after the rug is completed. Contemporary weavers create interesting variations in rya and flossa rugs by combining cut pile with loops, weft floats, and plain weave in the same piece. The hanging from Sweden shown in figure 5-15 consists of basically horizontal bands of off-white, gray, yellow, orange, brown, purples, blues, and greens and is a lively example of this special approach.

Another technique was used by Val Krohn-Ching of Hawaii to interpret an ancient warrior's helmet from the Bishop museum in Honolulu. Taking inspiration from Hawaiian feather art, she wrapped 22,000 tassels individually and wove them into the background to create *Mahiole* a 300-pound wall piece commissioned by the Hawaii State Foundation on Culture and the Arts in 1974 (fig. 5-16 and 5-17).

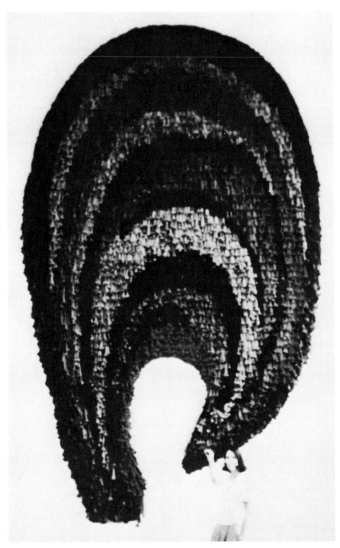

Skulato or Pulled-up Loops for Pile Weaves

Geometric pile textiles are often constructed by pulling up loops between warp threads instead of knotting them into the background (fig. 5-18). This method has been used from ancient Egypt and Peru to modern times to achieve geometric designs in pile weave. In Greece this method is called Skulato. Related to rug-making techniques, but not as durable as knotting, pulled-up pile is most often used for bags and other accessories.

The weave must be very firm and tight in order to hold the loops in place. Very attractive surface textures can be achieved by combining loops with flat, weft-faced background areas. The warp is sett at 20 ends per inch in wool or cotton. The weft is homespun wool, used double on the shuttle for the pile, single for the tabbies. Since the threading is plain weave, only two harnesses are needed. The loops are pulled up from right to left, or left to right, which gives them a slight slant. Three finer tabby threads are thrown between each row of loops and beaten very hard before the next row is started. Loops may be pulled up with the fingers or a crochet hook and are placed on a rod, whose circumference determines the size of the loops. When a thin rod, such as knitting needle, is used, it is best to weave several rows of loops with several rods before pulling out the first one. Groups of loops can be worked in individual areas, in which case the ends of the loop yarn can be turned around a warp thread or laid in with the background tabby. Loops may also be carried along with the ground weft from one area to another.

5-16. *Mahiole*, by Val Krohn-Ching; wall piece composed of 22,000 tassels. Commissioned by the Hawaii State Foundation on culture and the arts. (Photo courtesy of Val Krohn-Ching)

5-17. Details of figure 5-16.

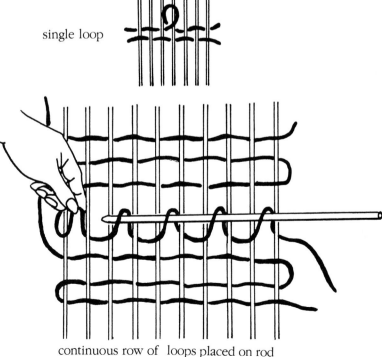

single loop

continuous row of loops placed on rod

5-18. Pulled-up loops

73

5-19. Wall hanging in Skulato technique; woven at the American Farm School in Thessaloniki, Greece. (Collection of the author; photo by Hector Garcia)

5-20. Detail of figure 5-19; material in black and white wool.

5-21. Greek bag with geometric designs in looped areas; home-spun wool on cotton warp. (Collection of the author; photo by Hector Garcia)

5-22. Greek bag with looped areas combined with diamond design in flat weave. (collection of the author; photo by Hector Garcia)

Figures 5-21 and 5-22 show examples of how this technique can be used for functional and decorative objects. Figures 5-23 and 5-24 show pile hangings made by using loom-woven overshots, which can be cut or left uncut for texture and color effects. (This technique, commonly called double corduroy, is explained at length in my book, *Weaving Sourcebook,* and in Peter Collingwood's *The Technique of Rug Weaving,* both listed in the Bibliography.)

5-23. *Blue Mood,* by Patricia Kreider; design made in pile and flat weaves. (Photo courtesy of Patricia Kreider)

5-24. *Brass Notes,* by Patricia Kreider; pile and flat weave areas in a hanging. (Photo courtesy of Patricia Kreider)

6-1. *Gris, Noir, Rouge,* tapestry designed by Jean Arp and woven at the Atelier Tabard Frères et Soeurs, Aubusson, France. (Photo courtesy of The Art Institute of Chicago)

Chapter 6

Designs in Tapestry Techniques

The ancient art of tapestry weaving has appeared in many shapes and forms throughout the world. It is one of the most versatile and beautiful forms of decorative textile arts, most expressive when executed in clearly defined sections of color. Tapestry weaving has been used for hangings and fabrics-from the boldest geometric designs to the finest naturalistic presentations, from the sturdiest rugs to the most delicate garments, in traditional, contemporary, and futuristic styles. Tapestries have been made for kings and for popes, for castles, churches, and royal households, and they are truly the culmination of the weaver's art. Characteristic of tapestry weaving is the weft-faced surface, usually in plain weave, with the designs defined by color changes within the boundaries of the shapes. The technique is very well suited to geometric shapes.

6-2. *Chelly Canyon,* by Alice Kawaga Parrott; wool and linen tapestry weave. (Photo courtesy of The Art Institute of Chicago)

The weave is basically simple: to cover the warp with the weft, the spaces between the warp threads must be wide enough for the weft to be beaten down. This is achieved by using a sett in which the spaces between warp ends are wider apart than the thickness of the weft yarns. In a rug of heavy wool, for example, a sett of 4 or 5 ends per inch may be enough, whereas in fine pictorial work as many as 15 or more ends per inch might be used.

The warp can be linen or cotton; the weft however, should be wool for flexibility and beauty. Color areas are worked as individual units, with each color wound on small bobbins or into butterflies. If the areas are carried in one line across the width of the warp, a beater is used; if they are not, the weft is beaten into place with a comb or fork. In laying in the weft, especially for large areas, it is important to "bubble" it to keep it sinuous and to prevent it from drawing in at the edges.

It is not within the scope of this book to give an exhaustive survey of the art of tapestry weaving. If you explore the techniques in samples however, you should have no difficulty acquiring a good understanding of possibilities and limitations. Samples may be woven spontaneously on the loom, but for large and important work, weavers usually use either full-size or reduced cartoons to establish design and color. Tapestries are traditionally woven sideways and with the back side facing the weaver, but the contemporary artist need not abide by these rules. Creative inspiration and less rigid requirements often yield most interesting results. Good craftsmanship and knowledge of technique, acquaintance with shapes and forms, coupled with understanding of colors and materials, assure a good background for creative expression.

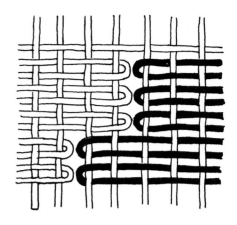

straight slit

Weaving Color Areas

Slit

There are many ways of laying the weft into the warp. The most common ones are shown in figure 6-3. In the slit method, colors in two adjoining areas meet but do not interlock. Each color returns to its side, leaving an opening space between the yarns. For long, straight lines, it is permissible to sew the slits together afterwards, but the method works best when used in small or diagonal lines.

Hatching

Two adjacent colors are woven back and forth in two alternating sheds for hatching, but in this case invade each other's space. This results in thin and feathery lines, which are very attractive as transitions from one color to the other.

Weft Interlocking Between Warp Threads

In this method, wefts of adjoining colors interlock with each other between warp threads, then return to their own side in alternating sheds.

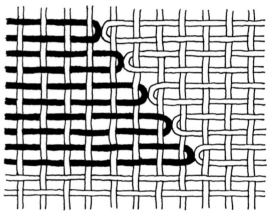

diagonal slit

Weft Interlocking Over Common Warp Thread

Here, wefts of two adjacent areas are carried around a common warp thread before returning to their own area in alternating sheds. Edges in this joining produce a soft, feathery effect.

Molding and Shaping

Areas may be built up and outlined with different-color threads. Shaping and molding may be done by building up a triangular shape and pushing the weft into the desired shape with the fingers. Circular shapes are made by staggering the outline of the warp threads as needed.

Double Interlock Method

Figure 6-3 shows an interlocking method that is not frequently used, but that is a prominent feature of paisley shawls (chapter 3).

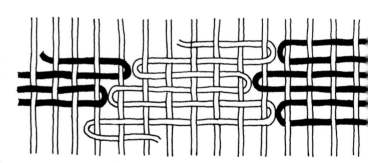

slit for three color areas

interlocking over a common
warp thread

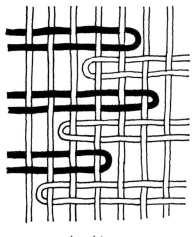

hatching

straight line dove-tailing

irregular dove-tailing

molding of curved areas

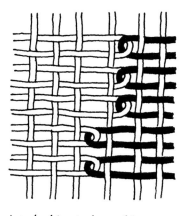

interlocking in the weft between
warp threads

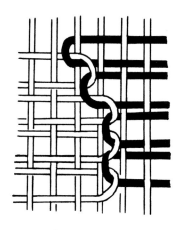

double interlock joining used in
paisley tapestry

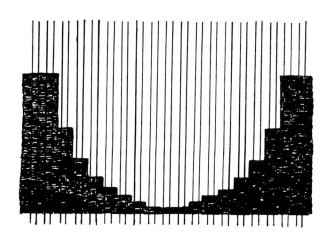

weaving a circle

6-3. Methods of tapestry weaving, joining of adjacent color areas (Diagrams by George Suyeoka)

6-4. *Chicago*, by Ann Williamson; small tapestry. (Photo courtesy of Ann Williamson)

Regeneration, by Martha Dean; hanging in soumak technique. (Photo courtesy of Martha Dean)

Detail of *Regeneration,* by Martha Dean. (Photo courtesy of Martha Dean)

Antique Persian Heriz Rug, mid-nineteenth century. (Photo by Otto E. Nelson; courtesy of Vojtech Blau Inc.)

Naksha-I-Gasata, by Philip E. Smith; rug in circle design. (Photo by Kirk S. Zutell)

Variation of *Woven Structures,* by Irene Suyeoka. (Photo courtesy of Irene Suyeoka)

83

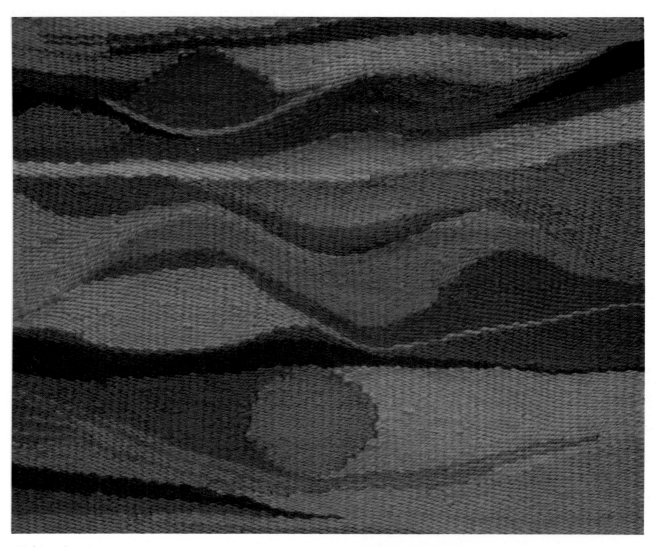

Multi colored tapestry sample by Jane Redman. (Photo courtesy of Jane Redman)

Woven Structures, by Irene Suyeoka. (Photo courtesy of Irene Suyeoka)

Design from Yugoslavia.
(Photo by Hector Garcia)

Triangular structure by Irene Suyeoka.
(Photo courtesy of Irene Suyeoka)

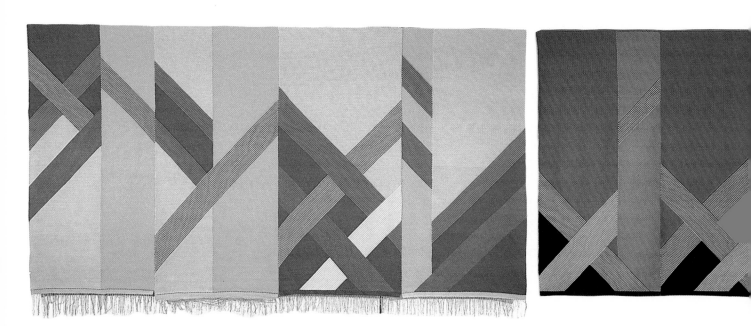

Passage to the Sea, by Charlotte Funk. Three panels: (A) Land,
(B) Sand, (C) Sea. (Photo courtesy of Charlotte Funk)

Soft Blocks, sculptural hanging in modular design by Ken
Weaver;. (Photo courtesy of Ken Weaver)

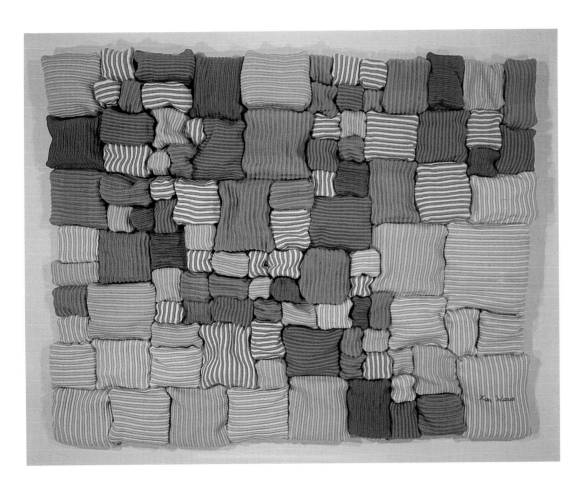

Geometric Tapestry II by Stephen Thurston. (Photo courtesy
of Stephen Thurston).

Mobius Progression, by Eunice B. Anders; woven structures.
(Photo courtesy of Eunice B. Anders)

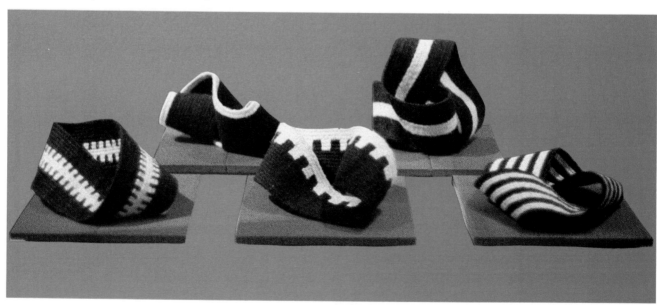

Guatemala Cross, hanging by Else Regensteiner. (Photo by Hector Garcia)

Cat. Pillow top from Peru. Stitchery on handwoven wool. (Photo by Hector Garcia).

89

Four Squares, by Philis Alvic; summer and winter weave. (Photo courtesy of Philis Alvic)

Reflections, by Philis Alvic; summer and winter weave. (Photo courtesy of Philis Alvic)

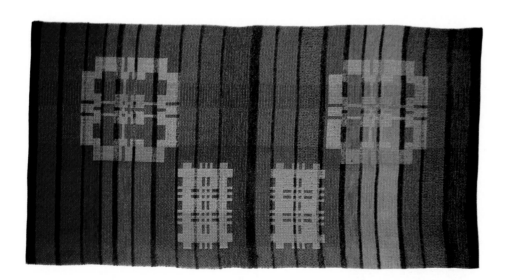

Double weave tree from Finland. (Photo by Hector Garcia.)

Reverse side of tree from Finland.

Opera Coat. Double weave by David Cress. (Photo courtesy of David Cress).

Modular design with supplementary warp by Irene Suyeoka. (Photo courtesy of Irene Suyeoka)

Variation in arrangement of modular design by Irene Suyeoka. (Photo courtesy of Irene Suyeoka)

Squares. Hanging in double weave by Irene Suyeoka. (Photo courtesy of Irene Suyeoka)

Reverse side of *Squares* by Irene Suyeoka. (Photo courtesy of Irene Suyeoka)

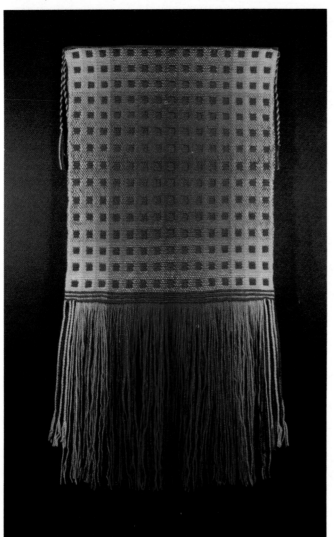

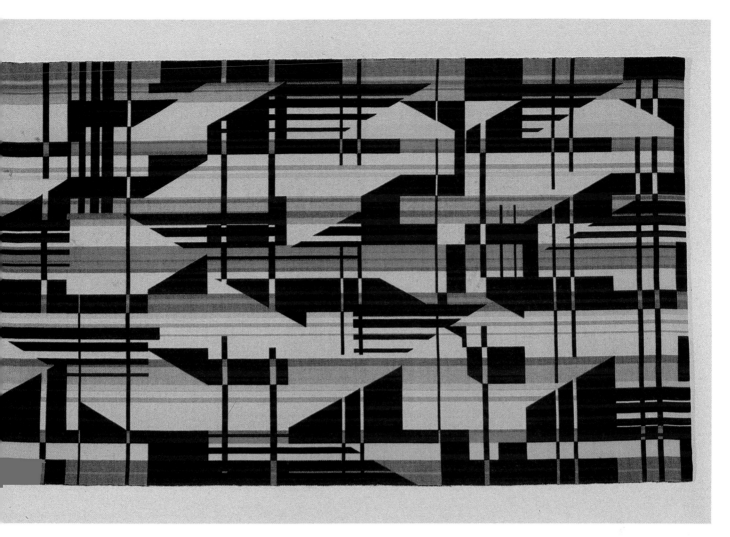

Remembered Traces. Double weave by Libby Kowalski.
(Photo courtesy of Libby Kowalski).

Detail of *Remembered Traces* by Libby Kowalski. (Photo
courtesy of Libby Kowalski).

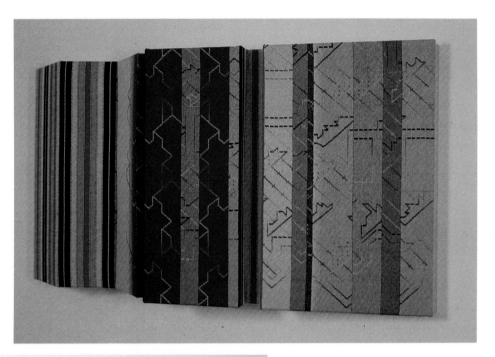

Splice, by Pat Kinsella; damask weave. (Photo courtesy of Pat Kinsella)

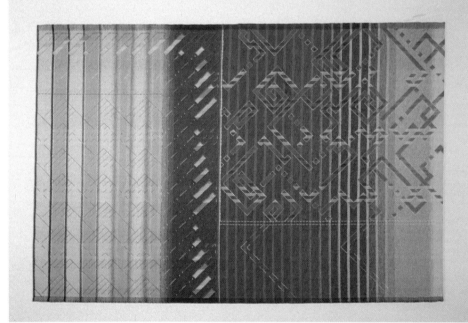

Deep End, by Pat Kinsella; damask weave. (Photo courtesy of Pat Kinsella)

Detail of *Deep End,* by Pat Kinsella. (Photo courtesy of Pat Kinsella)

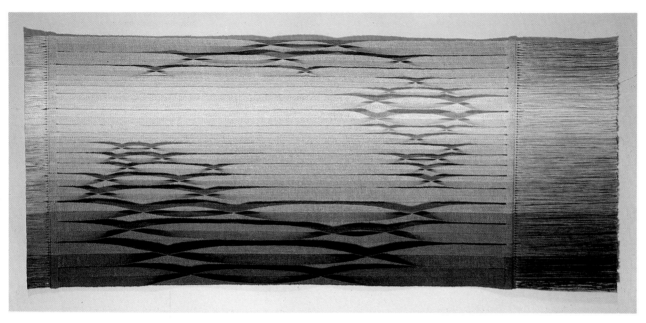

Winter Solstice, by Eunice B. Anders; double weave. (Photo courtesy of Eunice B. Anders)

The Leaves of Brown and Red and Yellow, by Eunice B. Anders; double weave. (Photo courtesy of Eunice B. Anders)

Detail of *The Leaves of Brown and Red and Yellow,* by Eunice B. Anders.

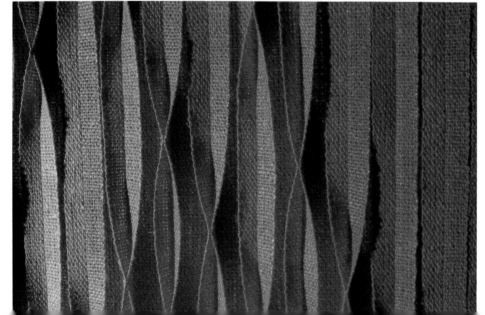

95

Collar from Guatemalan boy's shirt. (Photo by Hector Garcia)

Band in pick-up design on fabric from Guatemala. (Photo by Hector Garcia)

Block design in summer and winter weave by Mary Dinerstein. (Photo by George Suyeoka)

Ethnic Tapestry Weaving

The technique of tapestry appears and is applied in an amazing variety of forms and styles. Masters of the tapestry technique are the Navajo Indians, who have developed their own distinctive style in very beautiful flat-woven rugs, some famous of which are called "Two Grey Hills" (fig. 6-5). They were named for the trading post located between Shiprock and Gallup, New Mexico. These rugs were woven on upright frame looms. The weavers used handspun yarns and subtle color schemes: blacks, whites, grays, and shades of brown. The yarns were spun with black and white wool carded together for the gray, and brown and white carded together for the tan areas. Designs are strictly geometric, with the pattern reversed in the center to give a mirror image, a feature of tessellation, discussed in chapter 4. Three tapestry techniques-joining weft over common warp, interlocking in the weft, and slit in the diamond designs—are beautifully applied to give a smooth, flat surface.

The great variety possible in geometric tapestry design is demonstrated by examples from Greece (fig. 6-6).

6-5. Two Grey hills rug, woven by Daisey Tauglechee, Navajo Indian, 1960. (Photo courtesy of The Art Institute of Chicago)

6-6. Fragment in slit tapestry weave, from the Folk Art Museum, Thessaloniki, Greece. (Photo courtesy of Philip E. Smith)

Headbands from Guatemala (fig. 6-7) are woven in many variations of tiny geometric patterns. On warps of about 28 ends per inch, colorful figure are woven in various tapestry methods, using cotton, silk, or shiny rayon threads that are fine enough to cover even such closely sett warps. These long bands are wound into halos and are worn only by married women.

Beautiful tapestry fragments in strong geometric presentations are also found in museum collections. One example, found in a slit tapestry from Peru's central coast, dated circa A.D. 1300, is the charming, two-dimensional image of a fish shown in figure 6-9. Symbols of fertility are represented by little fish in its stomach.

6-7a. Headband worn by young woman at Lake Atitlan, Guatemala. Drawing by Irene Suyeoka.

6-7. Geometric designs in headbands from Guatemala. (Collection of the author; photo by Hector Garcia)

6-8. Monkey, tapestry from Ecuador. (Collection of the author; photo by Hector Garcia)

6-9. Fragment, cotton and wool slit tapestry weave; Peru, central coast, Chancay-Huarmey Culture, ca. 1300. (Photo courtesy of The Art Institute of Chicago)

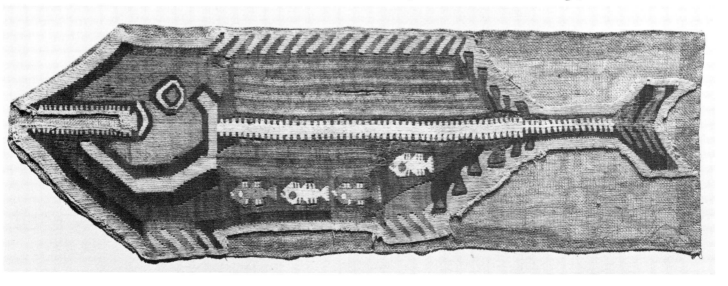

6-10. *Cliché—Triptych*, by Joanna Staniszkis; 1981; tapestry in wool, silk, and mohair on cotton warp. (Photo by Vida/Saltmarche, Toronto)

Contemporary Tapestry

Some important tapestries in traditional techniques have been designed by painters and executed in studios in various countries. For example, *Gris, Noir, Rouge,* (fig. 6-1), designed by Jean Arp, was woven at Aubusson, France. Another, a hanging showing Josephine Baker, was designed by and woven under the direction of Robert Brady; it was woven in wool tapestry in Cuernavaca, Mexico (fig. 6-11). Josephine Baker was a black American who emigrated to Paris in 1925 to become a celebrated singer and dancer in the French music halls. She became a star at La Revu Nègre and was famous for performing in a G-string ornamented with bananas, a costume in which she is depicted in Brady's tapestry. Other tapestries, such as the ones shown in figures 6-10 through 6-20, were designed and woven by the artists themselves. Diversions from traditional concepts of tapestry techniques are created in textured yarns, with warp and weft visible components of the design.

6-12. *Mouzieys Eco System,* sisal, wool, cotton, copper, and synthetic stilon; designed by Jolanta Owidzka and woven by Jolanta Owidzka with the assistance of Teresa Nunez, Poland, 1980. (Photo courtesy of The Art Institute of Chicago)

6-11. *Josephine Baker,* hanging in tapestry weave; designed by and woven under the direction of Robert Brady in Cuernavaca, Mexico, 1974. (Photo courtesy of The Art Institute of Chicago)

6-13. Hanging by Else Regensteiner. (Photo by Hector Garcia)

6-14. Tapestry by Larry Edman. (Photo courtesy of Larry Edman)

6-15. *African Mask,* tapestry by Napoleon Henderson. (Photo courtesy of Napoleon Henderson)

6-16. Tapestry by Napoleon Henderson. (Photo courtesy of Napoleon Henderson)

6-17. Geometric tapestry in black, white, and red, by Marie
Eckl. (Photo courtesy of Marie Eckl)

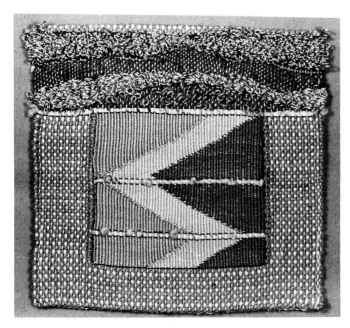

6-18. *Grand Illusions: Jupiter,* by Marjorie Durko Puryear; tapestry in wool, cotton, and silk with tufting. (Photo courtesy of Marjorie Durko Puryear)

6-19. *White Zip,* by Charlotte Funk; twill tapestry. (Photo courtesy of Charlotte Funk)

6-20. *American Diptych,* by Charlotte Funk; twill tapestry,
wool on cotton warp. (Photo courtesy of Charlotte Funk)

Meet-Cross-and Separate

An effect similar to tapestry is achieved by a method of weaving called "meet and separate" in which areas of color are woven so that one is kept dark, another light, and a third in a mixture of both shades, using them in alternating plain weave sheds. The method resembles slit tapestry in the arrangement of hatching, and geometric shapes can easily be woven by moving the meeting points according to the planned design.

Another method of creating interesting color areas uses dark, light, and mixed colors in plain as well as in striped horizontal and vertical combinations. Alternation of dark and light color picks results in a vertical area. When two dark and two light threads alternate in plain weave picks, horizontal lines are achieved. The light and dark threads are crossed at predetermined points in the design. (Further information can be found in my book, *Weaving Sourcebook: Ideas and Techniques,* as well as in Peter Collingwood's book, *The Technique of Rug Weaving,* listed in the Bibliography.)

An original variation of these techniques has been labeled "meet-cross-and separate" by artist-weaver Marilyn Holtzer. She says: "In *Iteration II* [6-22], I combined the method of meet and separate which gives areas of horizontal stripes between solid areas of two colors, with crossed wefts, which makes alternating areas of horizontal and vertical stripes. I call this method a hybrid of the two techniques."

6-21. *Gradations I,* by Marilyn E. Holtzer; hanging in meet-cross-and-separate technique. (Photo courtesy of Marilyn E. Holtzer)

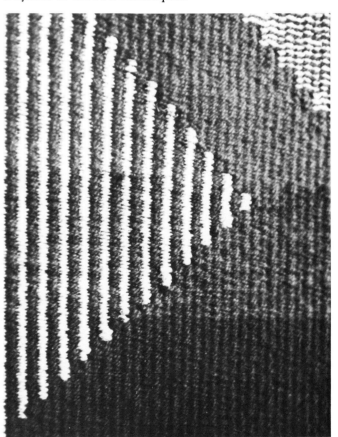

6-23. Detail of figure 6-22.

108

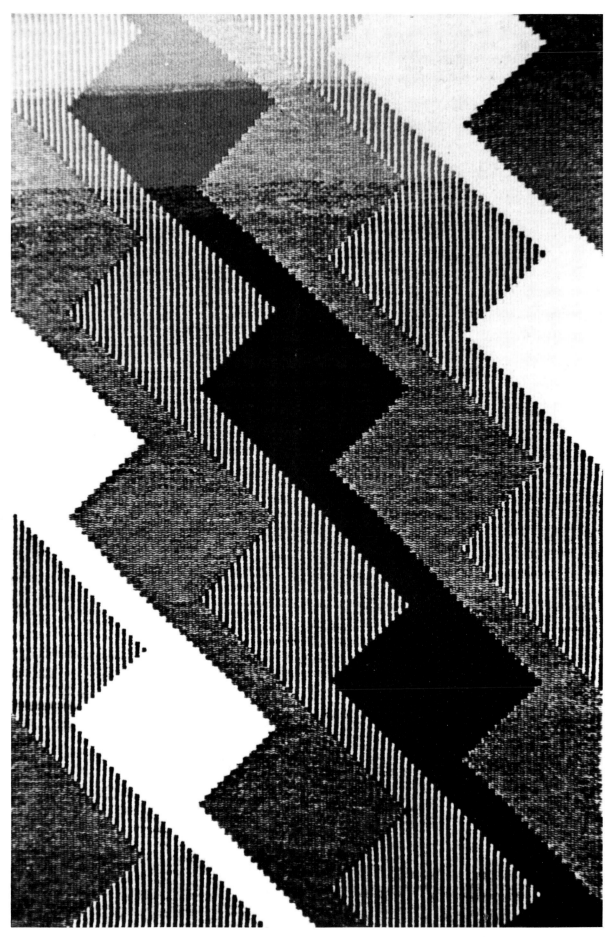

6-22. *Iterations II,* by Marilyn E. Holtzer; hanging in meet-cross-and-separate technique. (Photo courtesy of Marilyn E. Holtzer)

a.

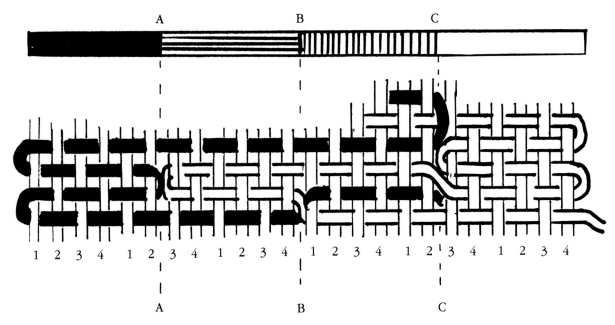

two colors, three junctions

b.

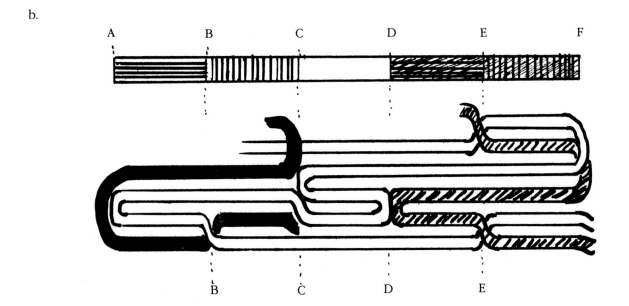

three colors, four junctions, five areas

c.

three colors, six junctions, seven areas

6-24. Three diagrams for meet-cross-and-separate methods (Diagrams by Marilyn E. Holtzer)

The simplest version of meet-cross-and-separate has two colors: four areas (solid light, horizontal stripes, vertical stripes, solid dark); and three junctions (A, B, and C between the four areas). The diagrams in figure 6-24 should make the crossings of light and dark colors quite clear. Using a third, preferably medium, color results in the seven areas shown in figure 6-24C.

It is important to keep changing the sheds as needed in order to maintain the plain weave order. Pieces in the hybrid technique should be woven wrong side up, and the design should be reversed accordingly.

6-26. Wall hanging by Jane Busse. (Photo couresty of Jane Busse)

6-25. Rug in meet-and-separate method by Jane Busse. (Photo courtesy of Jane Busse)

6-27. Wall hanging by Jane Busse; three-color meet-and-separate method. (Photo courtesy of Jane Busse)

Chapter 7

Designs in Laid-in and Pick-up Techniques

Fascinating textiles have been made with methods using extra warp or weft yarns. When these yarns are needed only for pattern and not for the general structure of the fabric, they are called *supplementary warps or supplementary wefts.* Weavers from such areas as Mexico, and Guatemala, Greece, and Scandinavia have a tradition of great skill in the weaving of such fabrics, and contemporary artists in all parts of the world make use of these techniques. Both functional and purely decorative textiles are made in stitchery, pick-up, laid-in, and brocaded weaves on primitive backstrap looms and four harness handlooms, as well as sophisticated draw- or dobby looms. All the methods used resemble each other, but each has definite characteristics of appearance and structure.

Laid-in Weaving

The structure of this weave consists of background and pattern. The pattern weft is laid into a shed together with or on top of a plain weave pick. While the background weft travels from selvage to selvage, the pattern weft moves back and forth only within its area of design. In another method, the pattern thread floats over the background and is tied down only by selected warp ends. Pattern threads are therefore carried on small shuttles or in butterflies.

Although patterns are rarely carried across the width of the warp, a pick-up stick is used when they are. This is a flat, smooth stick, approximately ½ inch wide and somewhat longer than the width of the warp. After the desired warp threads are placed on the stick, it is turned on edge and the pattern weft is inserted.

Pattern threads are usually heavier than the ground warp and weft as well as being of a different color. Many laid-in weavings are worked with the wrong side facing the weaver so that the turn of the pattern threads will not show on the right side.

Designs are drawn on graph paper, with one square representing one, two, or more warp threads.

Patterns are sometimes picked up on the closed shed, as illustrated in figure 7-4. In figure 7-5, several areas within the design are laid in while the plain weave background is woven with shuttles traveling from selvage to selvage. Other times, warps are picked up with the shed open, alternating the pick-up of selected threads on the even-numbered harnesses with pick-up on the odd-numbered sheds. The usual plain weave foundation tabbies are woven between each pattern pick. When picked-up pattern wefts travel under the same warp threads several times, vertical lines occur within the design area. This effect is also discussed in the section on Dukagang technique.

7-1. Cat in geometric design, stitchery on handwoven plain weave background. Twentieth century, Peru. (Collection of the author; photo by Hector Garcia)

7-2. *Rag Jacket,* by Gwynne Lott; inlay of rayon loop yarn. (Model, Elaine Sauer; photo courtesy of Gwynne Lott)

in plain weave shed

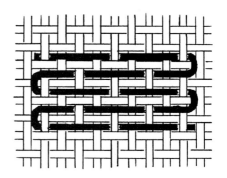

with surface floats

7-3. Weaving laid-in designs (Drawings by Irene Suyeoka)

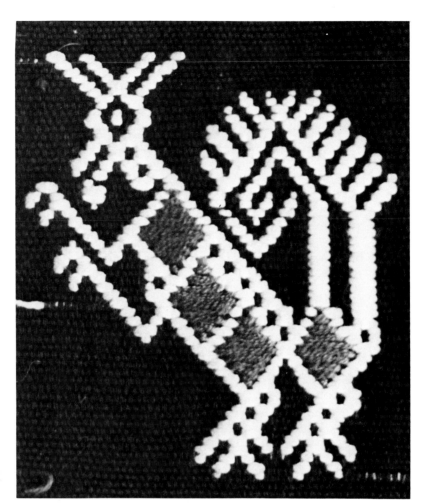

7-4. Weft pick-up designs from a Guatemalan fabric

stylized animal

diamond pattern

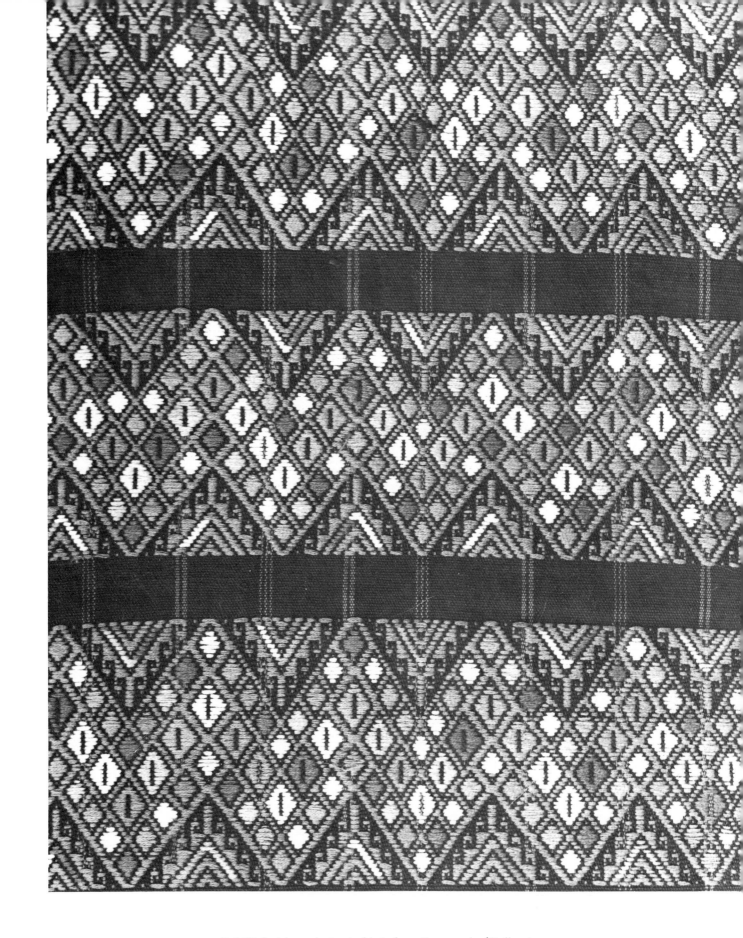

7-5. Weft pick-up design in fabric from Guatemala. (Collection of the author; photo by Hector Garcia)

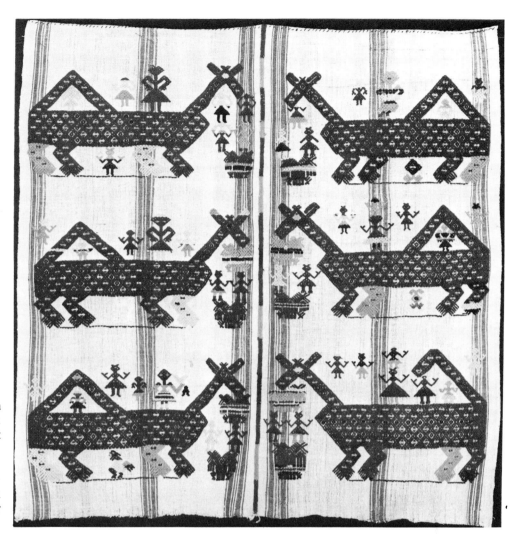

7-6. Carrying cloth (Tzut) from Guatemala, twentieth century. (Photo courtesy of The Art Institute of Chicago)

7-7. Brocaded collar from Guatemalan boy's shirt. (Collection of the author; photo by Hector Garcia)

7-8. Cotton fabric with bird, animal, and human figures in laid-in designs, woven in Guatemala. (Collection of the author; photo by Hector Garcia)

Frequently, intricate designs are combined with stripes or bands of loom-woven patterns. Diamonds, stars, stylized birds, and animal and human figures can appear in textiles of coarse wool material as well as of fine cotton fibers.

Modern technology has modified many of these traditional techniques for use on mechanical looms for commercial production. The machine-woven Greek bag in figure 7-11 is an example of such a textile. The intricate geometric design, strong color contrast, and closely woven cotton material make this bag a reasonably priced and attractive tourist item.

7-9. Geometric designs in pink, green, yellow, and rust wool, woven in Greece. (Collection of the author; photo by Hector Garcia)

7-10. Panel in brocading wefts and complementary weft stripes; late nineteenth to early twentieth century, Sweden. (Photo courtesy of The Art Institute of Chicago)

119

Warp Pick-Up

Many textiles from various countries have geometric patterns that are more suitable for use in a warp pattern than weft brocade. Two warps are planned and threaded: one for the foundation; the other, a supplementary warp, for the pattern pick-up. The foundation warp is sett very close, especially in Guatemalan and Peruvian fabrics, with as many as 80 ends of cotton warp per inch. The supplementary pattern warp has fewer threads per inch and is of coarser material than the foundation.

The supplementary pattern warp is often planned in color sections, while the foundation warp remains a natural color and, together with the tabby weft of the same yarn, forms a sturdy background. In the Peruvian bag shown in figure 7-12, the background warp and weft is a wool yarn of tightly spun singles; the pattern yarn is two-ply wool, 24 ends per inch. In fabrics with that many ends per inch and of narrow width (fig. 7-13), the reed is sometimes eliminated and the warp spread with two inserted sticks. When threaded on a handloom instead of the simple backstrap loom, the two warps should be put on separate warp beams; or the pattern warp can hang loose over the back of the loom, as shown in figure 7-15. Only three sheds are needed: the foundation warp can be threaded on harnesses 1 and 2, while the pattern warp goes on harness 3, or preferably on harnesses 3 and 4.

7-11. Machine-woven Greek bag in cotton warp and weft. (Collection of the author; photo by Hector Garcia)

7-12. Peruvian bag in warp pick-up technique with colored bands. (Collection of the author; photo by Hector Garcia)

For pick-up: 1. Raise the pattern warp. 2. Pick up the pattern with the pick-up stick. 3. Drop the pattern warp, but leave the stick in the warp. 4. Raise the first tabby and weave. 5. Raise the second tabby and weave. 6. Continue this treadling for as long as desired.

When changing the design, remove the pick-up stick and tie the pattern down by raising tabby harness 1 and weave, then tabby harness 2 and weave. Repeat the pick-up according to design

Since floats of the supplementary pattern warp occur in the places where the pattern does not appear on the surface, it is wise to design with this fact in mind.

120

7-13. Belt from Peru, first half of the twentieth century. (Photo courtesy of The Art Institute of Chicago)

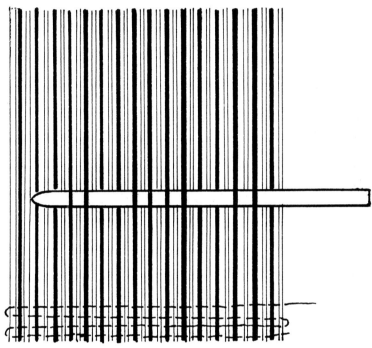

7-14. Pattern warp picked up on stick. (Drawing by Irene Suyeoka)

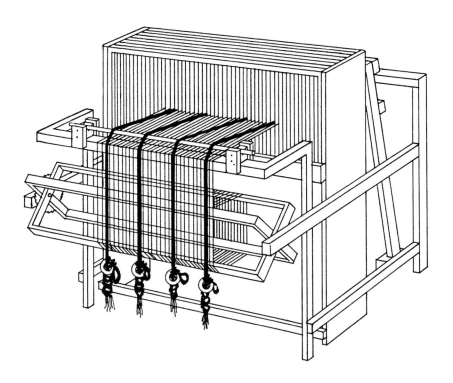

Handloom with supplementary warp placed over bar in back of the loom

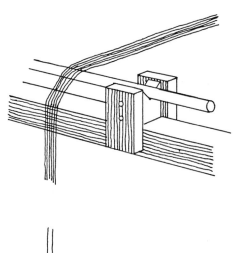

individual chains of supplementary warp weighted with washers

7-15. (Drawings by George Suyeoka)

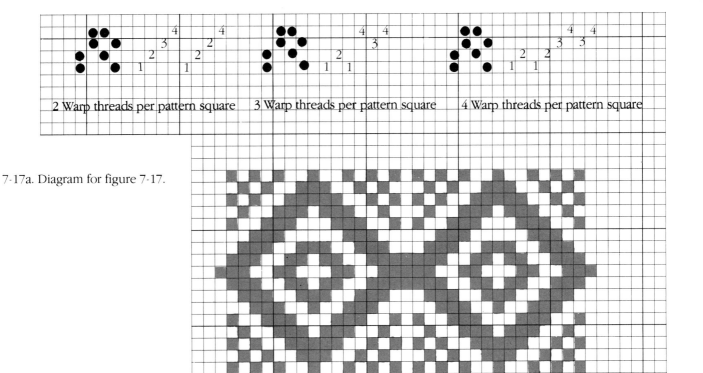

2 Warp threads per pattern square   3 Warp threads per pattern square   4 Warp threads per pattern square

7-17a. Diagram for figure 7-17.

Double Weave

When clear, contrasting shapes and strong designs are desired, few techniques prove as versatile and satisfying as double weave. The term *double weave* implies two fabrics, consisting of two warps and two wefts that are woven simultaneously one on top of the other.

Double cloth can be planned for a number of purposes, all woven by different methods:
- double cloth made in order to produce fabric of extra thickness.
- double cloth in which the two layers are joined at one selvage; this fabric can be unfolded to make a double-width material.
- double cloth in which the two layers are woven as separate pieces, one on top of the other.
- double cloth at which both layers are joined at each side to make a seamless tube.
- pick-up double weave, in which the two layers must be of contrasting colors and by which reversible designs can be woven.

Because I am concentrating on geometric design in this book, only pick-up and the tubular methods of weaving are presented. All other methods are discussed in *The Art of Weaving*, and *Weaving Sourcebook*. Loom-controlled double weaves are presented in chapter 10.

Double weave can be textured or plain, colorful or black and white, smooth or rough. Settings with fine threads and many threads per inch give a sharp, concise outline to geometric designs, while heavier yarns with texture and less ends per inch produce softer effects. The design can consist of bold shapes with large areas, or it can include fine lines and subtle color changes in warp and weft. No matter how the double weave is planned, the principal consideration must be the basic structure of the weave.

7-18. Pre-Columbian cloth in pick-up double weave on doll from Peru. (Collection of the author; photo by George Suyeoka)

Planning the Warp

In planning the warp, the same instructions are valid for both the tubular weave and the pick-up method, with only one difference: in order to produce a reversible design for the pick-up method the top and bottom layers must be planned in contrasting colors, while the tubular fabric may be effective when both layers are warped with same-color yarns. For double weave, the number of warp threads must be doubled. They are used single in the heddles, but doubled in the reed. On a four-harness loom, the two colors can be threaded alternately, with the first layer on harnesses 1 and 3 and the second layer on harnesses 2 and 4. In another version, the first layer can be threaded on harnesses 1 and 2 and the second layer on harnesses 3 and 4. Both systems require that the threads be doubled in the reed. When threaded alternately, outlines of the designs are smoother and steeper diagonals can be woven. Sizes of threads should be the same for both layers.

7-19. *Jerusalem,* by Dona Rosenblatt; hanging in pick-up double weave. (Photo courtesy of Dona Rosenblatt)

Pick-Up Double Weaves

Pick-up designs are made in contrasting colors for the top and the bottom layers. In the design, selected parts of the bottom layer can be brought to the surface, while the top colors from the same areas form the design on the reverse or underside in the weaving process. This method creates distinct positive and negative designs and is also sometimes called *Finnweave.*

Thread the loom in alternating colors, with the light colors on harnesses 1 and 3, dark on 2 and 4. The pattern should be worked out on graph paper, with filled-in squares representing the design. The design appears in the reverse color on the back side of the fabric. When the design is dark on a light background on one side, it will be light on a dark background on the other. Two shuttles, one wound with each color, and a pick-up stick are needed. The weaving procedure is as follows:

1. Raise harnesses 2 and 4 (dark warp); with the beater at rest position (away from you), slide the point of the pick-up stick over and under the dark warp threads, picking up all design threads indicated in the first (bottom) row of the graph paper plan. This will give you the dark design on the light background. When the stick is inserted for the full width of the warp, slide it (with its picked-up threads) back against the reed, letting it ride on top of the shed. Release treadles.

2. Treadle harness 1, which raises the first half of the light layer. Weave with light weft. Beat without removing the stick. Slide the stick back against the reed again. Release the treadle.

3. Treadle harness 3 to raise the other half of the light warp. Weave light. Take out the pick-up stick and beat. Always be sure to leave a wide arc of weft in the shed for good edges.

4. Treadle 1 and 3 (all light warp threads). With the stick, pick up the background threads that were just woven, as indicated in the graph, again working from right to left. Release treadles.

5. Treadle harness 2, and weave with the dark weft. Beat as well as possible with the stick in position. Slide the stick against the reed. Release the treadle.

6. Treadle harness 4, and weave dark. Remove the pick-up stick and beat. This completes one set of pick-up. If the woven design does not make a square with two picks in each layer for each row of the graph, use as many sets of the same picks as necessary to complete the proper proportions.

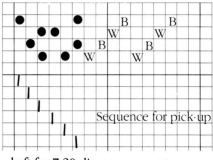

7-20. Pick-up draft for 7-20 diagram on next page.

Tubular Weaves

The easiest tubular weave requires only one shuttle, which goes around and around from the top layer to the bottom and back. The warp must consist of an odd number of threads to prevent adjacent threads at the edges from being woven alike. Shaping and stuffing of the tubes (fig. 7-21) creates a three-dimensional design, but the weave can also be more functional, as when used for bags and pillows.

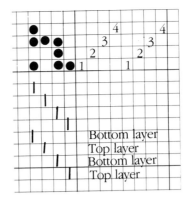

Bottom layer
Top layer
Bottom layer
Top layer

7-20. Draft and diagram of tubular double weave.

7-21. Tubular wallpiece by Karen Hanson. (Photo courtesy of Karen Hanson)

127

7-22. *Remembered Traces,* by Libby Kowalski; double cloth in cotton and linen. (Photo courtesy of Libby Kowalski)

7-23. Detail of figure 7-22.

7-24. *Flowers for Lyra,* by Libby Kowalski; double cloth in linen and cotton. (Photo courtesy of Libby Kowalski)

7-25. Detail of figure 7-24.

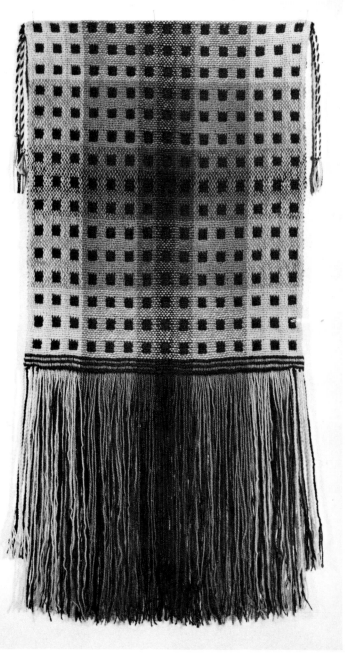

7-27. *Squares and Spaces Series #3,* by Marjorie Durko Puryear; double weave with stitchery. (Photo courtesy of Marjorie Durko Puryear)

7-26. *Squares,* by Irene Suyeoka; wall hanging in double weave. (Photo courtesy of Irene Suyeoka)

130

Wallhangings in Double Weave

Many contemporary weavers enjoy the strong contrasts of black and white reversible designs, where shapes and patterns stand out in clear, hard-edged lines. This conception of geometric design is shown in the composition of light and dark areas by Libby Kowalski (fig. 7-24 and 7-25). In stunning arrangements, shapes, lines, proportions, relationships of pattern, background, and weave structure work together beautifully for a very satisfying visual statement.

When bright colors in both layers are used, the effect becomes different and exciting, and the geometric shapes assume a texture of their own. Irene Suyeoka achieved this effect in *Squares* by shading the warp from gold-yellow to orange-red for one layer, and blue for the other layer (fig. 7-26). The reversible hanging is predominantly blue on one side and brilliant yellow-red on the other side.

A different feeling is expressed in a series of hangings by Marjorie Durko Puryear, for which she combines double weave in linen yarns with stitchery (fig. 7-27 and 7-28). She says: "The aspects of geometric stylization that I have been exploring are developed through personal design philosophy as affected by the structure of weaving. Stylization of imagery is more important than the simplistic woven plane."

7-28. *Green Spaces,* by Marjorie Durko Puryear; double weave with stitchery. (Photo courtesy of Marjorie Durko Puryear)

Double-faced Rugs in Pick-up Technique

Weft-faced rugs, based on alternation of contrasting colors in the weft, can be woven by double weave pick-up methods, as illustrated in the example by Sadye Tune Wilson shown in figure 7-29. The warp is of 8/5 linen, warped to make 5 double threads per inch in heddles and reed. Weft is heavy 3-ply wool used double on the shuttles. Threading is straight twill on only three harnesses. The artist gives the following directions for weaving:

The treadling sequence for the pattern area is:

1. Raise harness 3. with the stick, pick up *pattern* warps according to the planned design. Lower harness 3. Push the stick against the reed. Raise harness 1. Weave weft of background color. Remove the pick-up stick. Drop harness 1.

2. Raise harness 3. With the stick, pick up *background* warps according to the planned design. Lower harness 3. Push the stick against the reed. Raise harness 1. Weave pattern color. Remove the pick-up stick. Drop harness 1.

3. Raise harness 3. With the stick, pick up *pattern* warps. Lower harness 3. Push the stick against the reed. Raise harness 2. Weave background color. Remove the stick. Drop harness 2.

4. Raise harness 3. Pick up *background* warps with the stick. Lower harness 3. Push the stick against the reed. Raise harness 2. Weave pattern color. Remove the stick. Drop harness 2.

The four picks beat into line to form one row on the face and one row on the reverse side of the rug.

For a treadling sequence for solid color areas from selvage to selvage:

1. Raise harnesses 1 and 3. Weave weft of the background color.

2. Raise harness 1. Weave weft of the pattern color.

3. Raise harnesses 2 and 3. Weave weft of the background color.

4. Raise harness 2. Weave weft of the pattern color.

The four picks beat into line to form one row on the face and one row on the reverse side of the rug. Design and background colors are reversed on the back of the rug.

7-29. Reversible rug in pick-up technique, by Sadye Tune Wilson. (Photo courtesy of Sadye Tune Wilson)

8-2. Details of figure 8-1.

132

Part III
Loom-controlled
Techniques

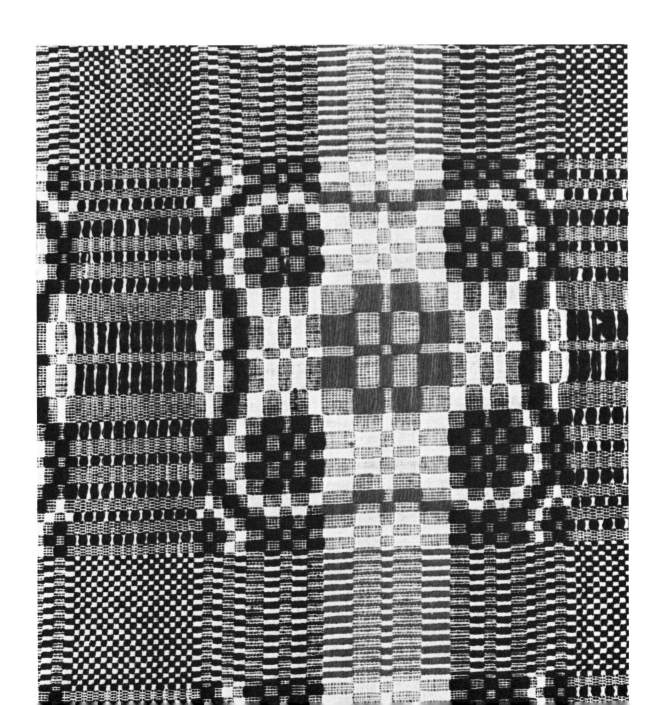

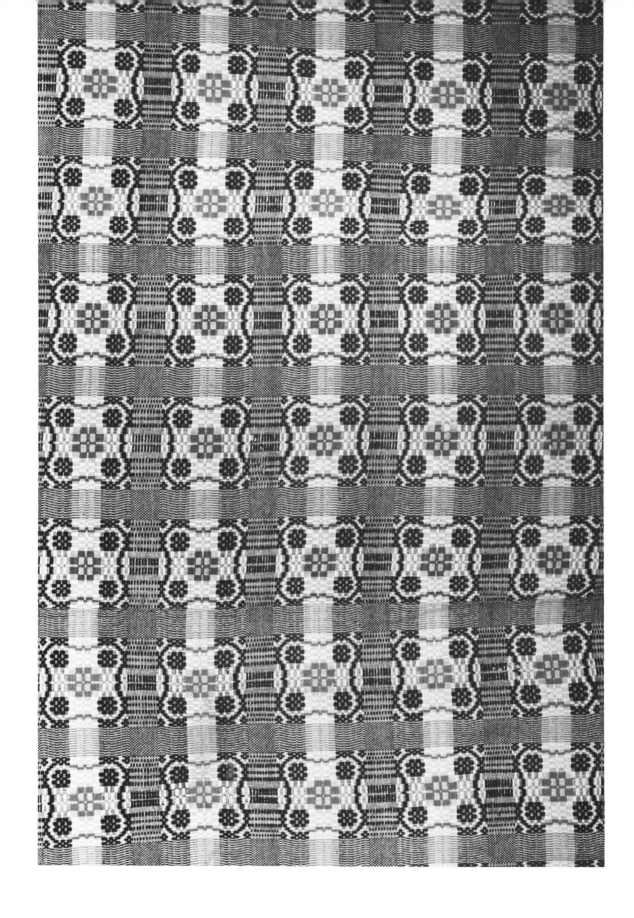

8-1. Coverlets, Whig Rose variation; woven by Sallie Alexander Zellner. (Photo courtesy of Sara English, granddaughter, and Sadye Tune Wilson)

Chapter 8

Designs in Overshot and Twill Weaves

Some of the best-known interpretations of geometric pattern weaves in traditional textiles are colonial coverlets. Brought to America from Europe these patterns were produced in great variety from the latter part of the eighteenth century to near the end of the nineteenth century, first in handwoven coverlets and later on multiharness and Jacquard looms. The inclusion of the weaver's or owner's name in the borders of the textile shows the importance assigned to them by the colonial families.

Handwoven coverlets are rare and hard to find today, but museum collectors and curators are conscious of their historical significance and efforts are being made by textile researchers to find and document coverlets owned, used, or preserved as heirlooms in private families. One such researcher is Sadye Tune Wilson, who has collected much information on coverlets in Tennessee and published it in her book, *Of Coverlets: the legacies, the weavers.*

Handwoven coverlets made by the women of rural households, as well as by professional weavers were woven with home-spun and often plant-dyed wool yarns on cotton warps in a variety of structures.

These coverlets represent an enormous variety of threading arrangements, profile drafts, and treadling modifications, resulting in beautiful and always well-balanced geometric designs. Pattern names are often indicative of their graphic arrangements: Whig Rose, Blooming Leaf, Snowballs, and Pioneer Trail, for example. Geometric designs, whether for overshot or for other systems of weave construction, are frequently presented graphically by a profile, or short, draft (fig. 8-3). This method is very useful, especially in threading systems involving blocks and units of threading. Instead of showing each individual thread drawn through a heddle, a group of threading units is indicated by filled-out squares on graph paper, in which each square represents inches or the number of times a unit is repeated across the design. For a complete picture, threading units of the warp and treadling repeats of the weft are shown. The weaver transfers this draft into an actual threading plan, such as overshot, summer and winter, or double weave structures.

8-3. Diagrams of profile drafts

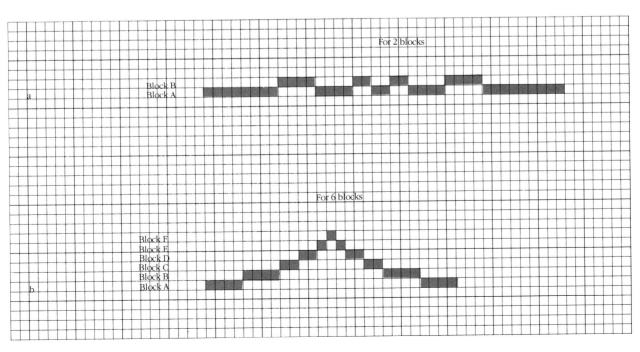

Overshot

Overshot was especially popular among colonial weavers because a variety of geometric designs could be created on a four-harness loom. Characteristic of the threading system are the overlapping threads, in which the last thread of one group is the beginning thread of the adjacent group. A supplementary pattern weft of heavier yarn alternates with a plain weave pick of finer thread, usually of the same size as the warp.

In weaving, the pattern weft skips over a group of warp threads while the alternating tabby in between each pattern pick gives a firm foundation. The inter-weaving of the pattern and tabby wefts with the threading arrangement creates three visual areas:

1. Solid areas where the pattern weft covers the background.

2. Solid areas showing the plain weave background.

3. A half-tone area formed by the combination of pattern weft and plain weave background. All three areas weave across simultaneously from selvage to selvage.

The system of threading is shown in figure 8-4. The standard tie-up is: 1-2, 2-3, 3-4, and 4-1. Tabbies are 1-3 and 2-4.

There are two versions of weaving:

1. Weaving the pattern in *Star Fashion*, also called *Weaving as drawn in* or, in older books, *Tromp as Writ*, means following the weaving draft used in the threading sequence. If each combination is squared in the number of warp and weft threads and is used in the same order as the draft, the pattern forms a diagonal of 45 degrees.

2. A change in the treadling sequence of the same pattern creates a variation called *Rose Fashion*:

Combination of harnesses 1-2 changes to 2-3
Combination of harnesses 2-3 changes to 3-4
Combination of harnesses 3-4 changes to 1-4
Combination of harnesses 1-4 changes to 1-2.

The order of treadling remains the same as before, and each combination must also be squared.

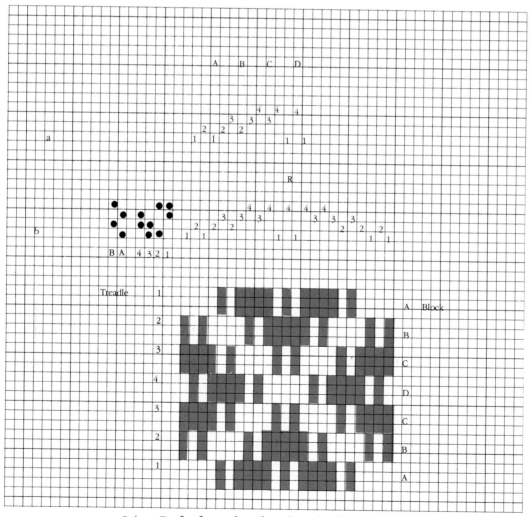

8-4. a. Draft of overshot threading; b. diagram of overshot pattern. (By Irene Suyeoka)

Monk's Belt

This is the name of a third version frequently used in overshot designs. It is also described as *weaving on opposites* and the principle is as follows:

Combination of harnesses 1-2 is followed by 3-4
Combination of harnesses 2-3 is followed by 1-4
Combination of harnesses 3-4 is followed by 1-2
Combination of harnesses 1-4 is followed by 2-3.

Although weaving on opposites can be used in many different threading variations and yarn and color changes, the tradition has established that each pattern pick is followed by a pick of background color on the opposite set of harnesses.

Margaret Windeknecht's rug, *Keep Out of the Cave* (fig. 8-5), was woven on eight harnesses with a 6/3 linen carpet warp, sett at 6 ends per inch. Pattern weft is a single-ply wool. The drafts and diagrams shown in figure 8-5a explain how the design was created.

8-5. *Keep Out of the Cave,* by Margaret Windeknecht; rug in monk's belt pattern. (Photo courtesy of Margaret Windeknecht)

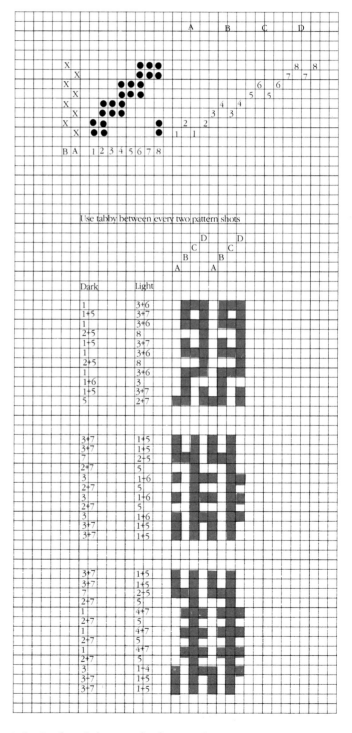

8-5a. Draft and diagram for figure 8-5.

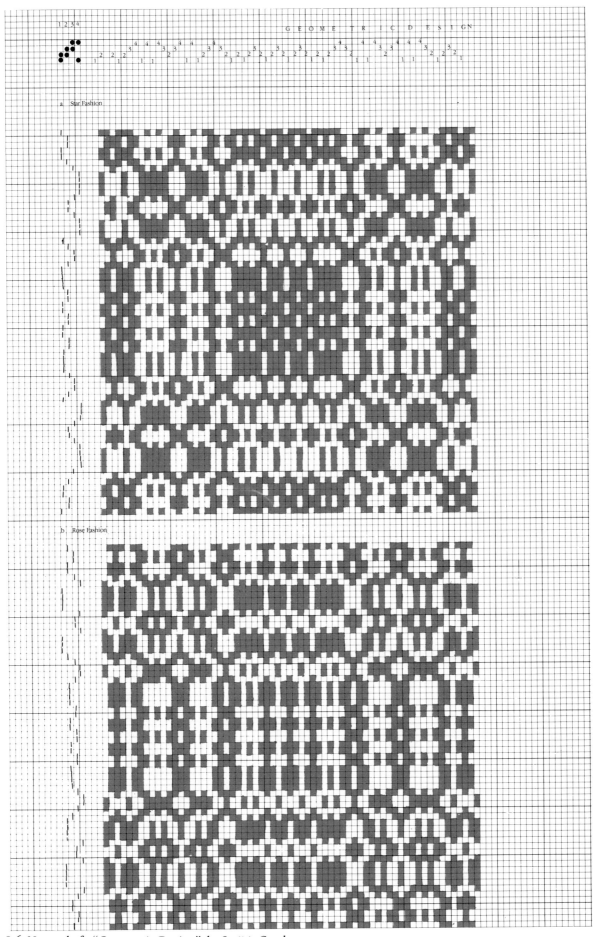

8-6. Name draft, "Geometric Design", by Judith Gordon.

Name Drafts

A most personal touch may be given to a weaving by transferring the letters of the alphabet to the heddles threaded on various harnesses. The weaver's own or any other name, can be transferred to the threading draft and executed in overshot or twill patterns. There are many possibilities for 4 or multiple harness weaves, and the designer should use the name draft only as a starting point for creating original patterns. With a chart established, the designer decides what other harnesses should be threaded along with those dictated by the chosen name.

Judith Gordon has designed an interesting four-harness overshot which she calls "Geometric Design" (fig. 8-6). She kindly supplied these directions:

1. Make a chart to establish the harness for each letter of the alphabet.

A	E	I	M	Q	U	Y	= Harness 1
B	F	J	N	R	V	Z	= Harness 2
C	G	K	O	S	W		= Harness 3
D	H	L	P	T	X		= Harness 4

2. Establish the harnesses used in the name "Geometric Design": G = harness 3, E = harness 1, O = harness 3, M = harness 1, and so on.

3. For the above name, skip a thread between each letter in the threading draft. Then return and fill in the harnesses, up or down, whichever you choose for the next thread to go on. Between letters that require it, add two extra threads in order to make a better pattern. After the completed name is drawn in, reverse the draft at the center point to get a balanced design.

Figure 8-6 shows the pattern woven in both star and rose fashion. (The changes in these treadling systems were explained previously in this chapter).

In another example by Barbara Engle Gent, the weaver's name was interpreted in a small woven hanging (fig. 8-7). Both versions, star and rose fashion, turned out to be successful geometric patterns.

8-7. Overshot sample based on artist's name, by Barbara Engle Gent. The top is woven rose fashion, the bottom star fashion. (Photo George Suyeoka)

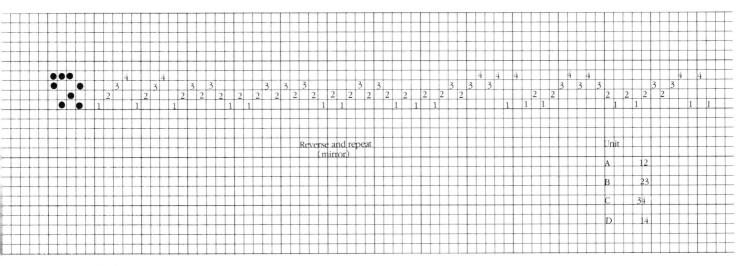

8-7a. Diagram for figure 8-7.

Eight-harness Twill

The alphabetical numbers change significantly on eight harnesses. Eleanor Best also chose the name "Geometric Design" for a name draft (fig. 8-8), and kindly supplied the following directions:

1. In this eight-harness twill, each letter of the alphabet is assigned a number from 1 to 26: A = 1, B = 2, C = 3, and so on. For the words "Geometric Design", G = 7, E = 5, O = 15, M = 13, E = 5, T = 20, R = 18, I = 9, C = 3, D = 4, E = 5, S = 19, I = 9, G = 7, N = 14. The alphabet numbers do *not* serve as harness numbers, but as guide numbers.

2. The first squence is established by *ascending* the twill to the first guide number, which is G = 7.

3. The last harness of that sequence becomes the first harness for the next sequence, E = 5, which has to *descend* for five threads, ending on harness 3.

4. The next group, O = 15, theoretically must go up for 15 threads. However, on eight-harness loom, it is necessary to go up to 8 and then return to harness 1 and continue the ascending line. The fifteenth thread is on harness 1 again.

5. For the next sequence, M = 13, the line must descend as shown in the draft.

This system offers multiple choices, enabling the weaver to design interesting, intricate, and personalized patterns on any given number of harnesses.

8-8. Name draft, "Geometric Design", for eight harnesses; designed by Eleanor Best, diagram by Judith Gordon.

141

Shadow Weaves

There are some color-and-weave effects, such as the log cabin or the houndstooth check, with which every weaver is familiar. Shadow weaves are related to these patterns insofar as alternating light and dark color in warp, in weft, or in both have a definite influence on the appearance of many weaves. Twills, block patterns, overshot, and other threadings and weaves are changed by this method. In a way, any pattern can be made into a shadow weave by this alternation of light and dark colors and will assume a different and sometimes even mysterious character. Designs usually look more diluted, as can be observed in Irene Suyeoka's name draft (fig. 8-9); strong squares are converted into a soft, textured all over surface design.

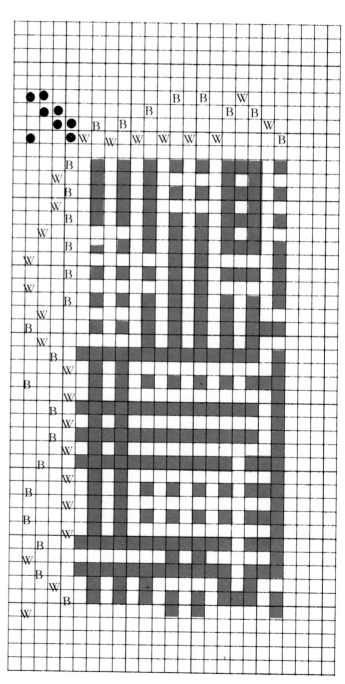

8-9a. Draft and diagram for figure 8-9.

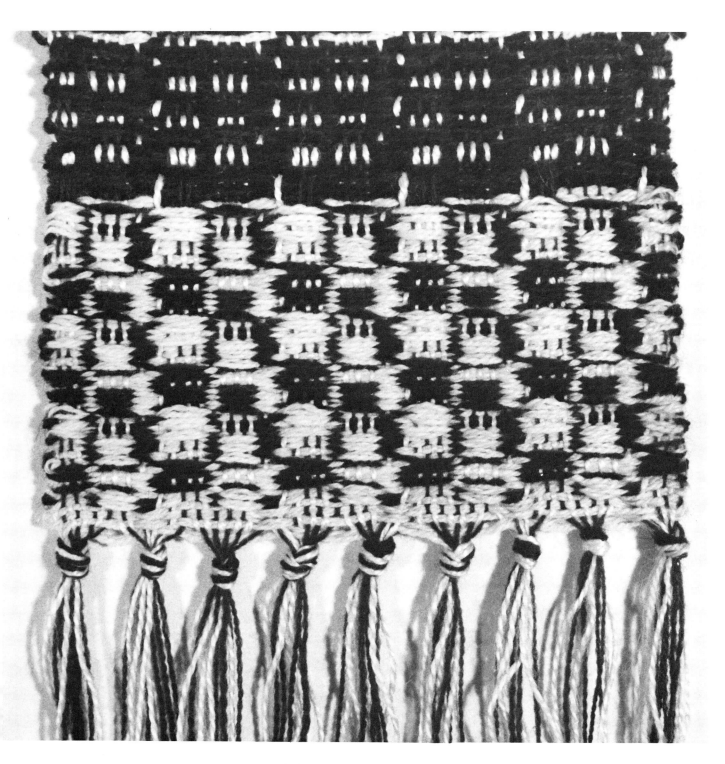

8-9. Name draft "Suyeoka" in shadow weave, by Irene Suyeoka. Some threads were added for a better pattern.

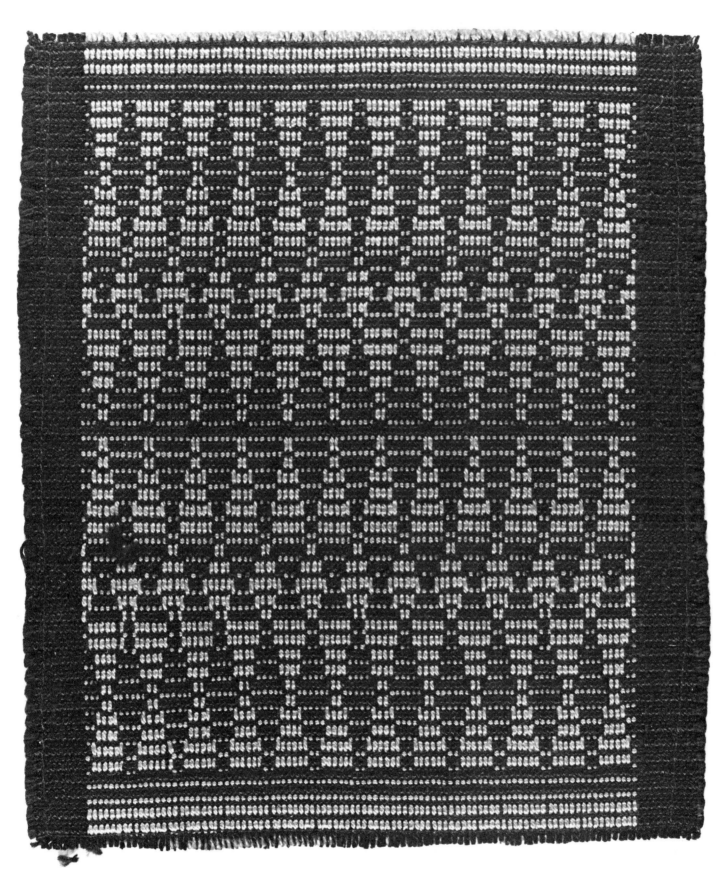

8-10. Warp-faced shadow weave by Jane A. Evans. (Photo by Bernard Gordon)

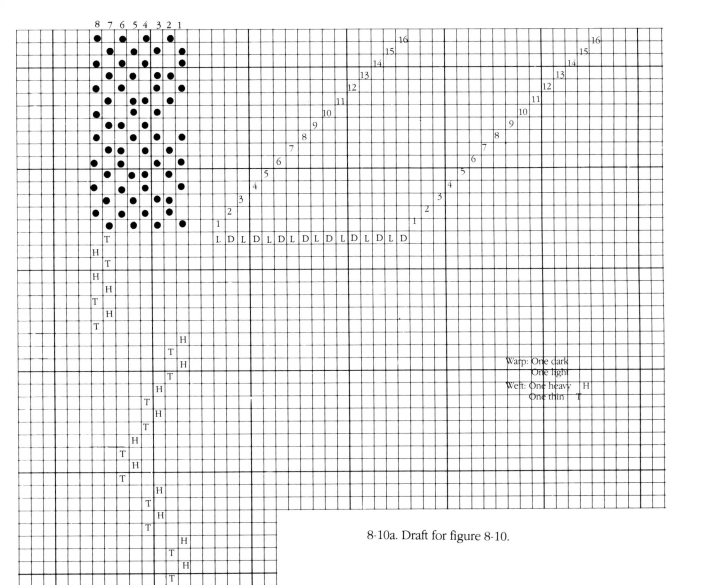

8-10a. Draft for figure 8-10.

Color is not the only factor that influences geometric pattern: another is the alternation of thick and thin yarns. A subtle shadow weave effect was achieved in a fabric woven on a 16-harness twill threading (fig. 8-10). Using an alternating warp of brown and red 10/2 cotton, weaver Jane A. Evans sett the warp closely at 48 ends per inch in a 12-dent reed. The weft alternates between fine (16/2) and heavier (8/8) black cotton yarn. The close setting of the warp resulted in a warp-faced fabric, a weave often called *Mattor* or warp-faced shadow weave. Jane Evans explains this structure: "This threading can be thought of as blocks, with neighboring odd and even harnesses making up one block. Therefore the combinations 1-2, 3-4, etc., constitute the blocks. In the threading they could be expanded into as many repeats of each block as desired. This weave can also be used on any number of harnesses, allowing two harnesses per block". It is interesting to see how flexible a straight twill threading can be. The border stripes in all-brown warp indicate further flexibility. Weft sizes can also be varied for more pattern changes.

8-11. *If There Is Magic,* hanging by Margaret Windeknecht. (Photo courtesy of Margaret Windeknecht)

The shadow weave effect is also prominent in the double-woven eight-harness hanging *If There is Magic* by Margaret Windeknecht (fig. 8-11). The threading, treadling, and double weave diagrams explain the technique behind this exciting and unusual design.

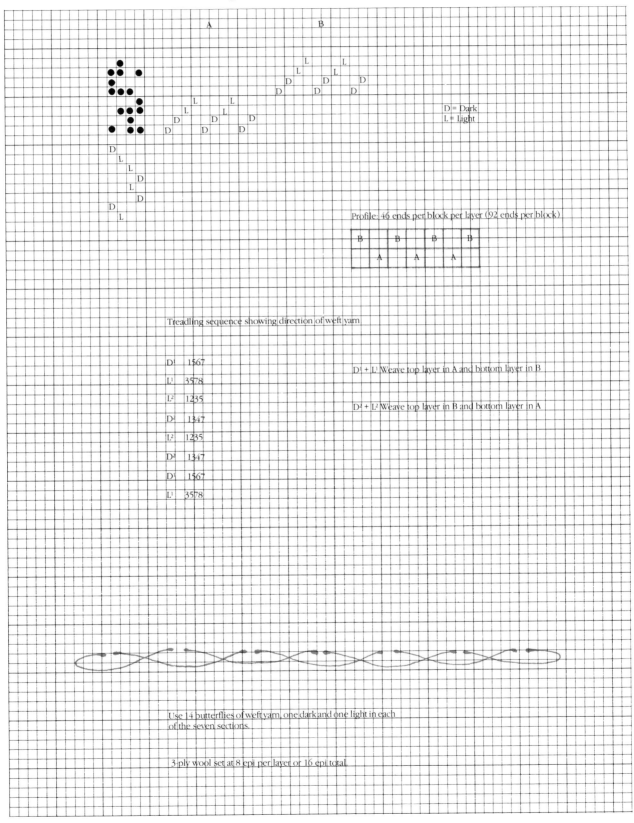

Profile: 46 ends per block per layer (92 ends per block)

D = Dark
L = Light

Treadling sequence showing direction of weft yarn

D¹	1567
L¹	3578
L²	1235
D²	1347
L²	1235
D²	1347
D¹	1567
L¹	3578

D¹ + L¹ Weave top layer in A and bottom layer in B

D² + L² Weave top layer in B and bottom layer in A

Use 14 butterflies of weft yarn, one dark and one light in each of the seven sections.

3-ply wool set at 8 epi per layer or 16 epi total.

8-11a. Draft and diagram for figure 8-11.

8-12. Ogee design by Barbara Gent. (Photo by George Suyeoka)

One of the most graceful geometric designs is that based on the ogee lines. An excellent combination of this design and the shadow weave concept is presented in Barbara Gent's woven piece (fig. 8-12). It is based on a draft from a small volume on shadow weaves, *1000+ Patterns in 4, 6, and 8 Harness Shadow Weaves* by Marian Powell.

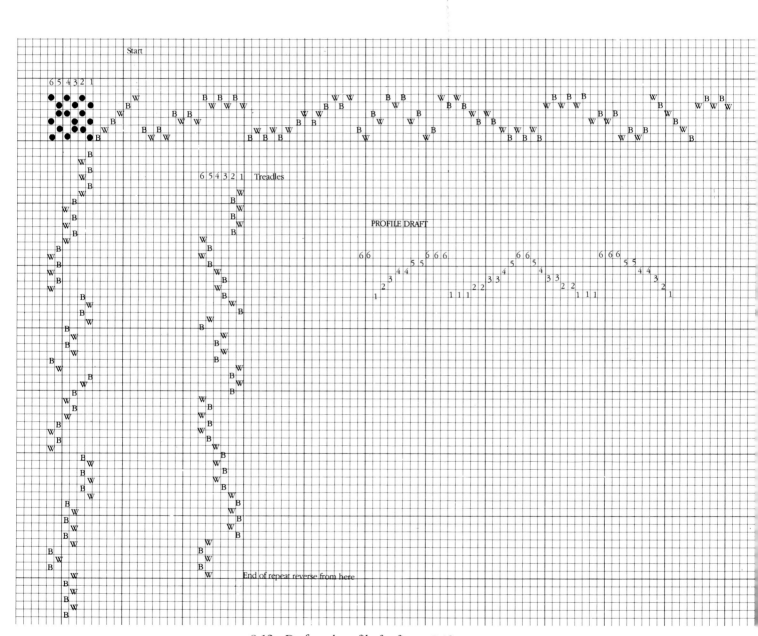

8-12a. Draft and profile for figure 8-12.

8-13. Navajo saddle blanket in bound weave by Jane A. Evans.
(Photo by Bob Hewitt)

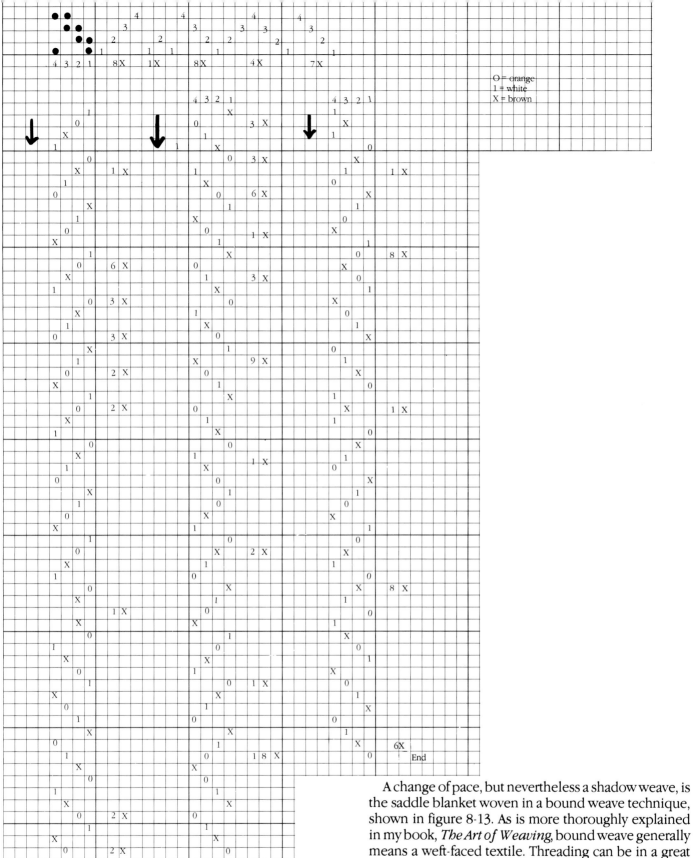

8-13a. Draft for figure 8-13.

A change of pace, but nevertheless a shadow weave, is the saddle blanket woven in a bound weave technique, shown in figure 8-13. As is more thoroughly explained in my book, *The Art of Weaving*, bound weave generally means a weft-faced textile. Threading can be in a great variety of patterns, of which the most frequently used are twill arrangements and twill adaptations. The warp of cotton or linen thread must be sett wide enough apart for the weft to cover it. The attractive Navajo-type saddle blanket shows many pattern variations made by treadling and by alternating wool yarns of light, dark and medium colors in the weft.

151

8-14. Geometric pattern in eight-harness twill by Judith Gordon.

152

8-14a. Draft and diagram for figure 8-14 by Judith Gordon.

Multi-harness Twills

Almost every weaver is well acquainted with the system and appearances of basic twills. The characteristic diagonal lines of simple four-harness twills or the exciting traces composed of many parallel lines possible on the eight-harness loom, the reversed twills, herringbone and diamond patterns, broken twills and undulating twills—all have been the basis for many geometric designs. Less frequently found are twill designs woven on handlooms of more than eight harnesses. A group of weavers named "The Sixteens" explores, designs, and weaves multi-harness structures and exchanges experiences and results with each other. In one such project, 16-harness straight twill threadings were used exclusively, and the amazing variations of four versions with the same threading are illustrated in figures 8-15 to 8-18. The drawdowns, constructed by Judith Gordon, show clearly the structures of the geometric designs achieved through tie-up, treadling, and color changes.

153

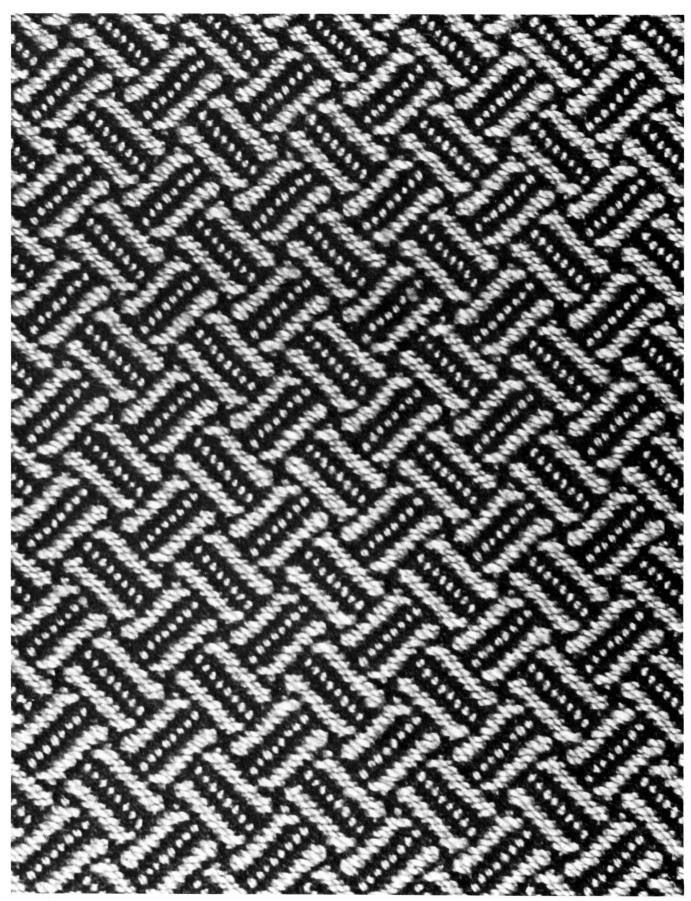

8-15. Plaited twill on sixteen harnessess, by Antonia Kormos.
(Photo by Bernard Gordon)

154

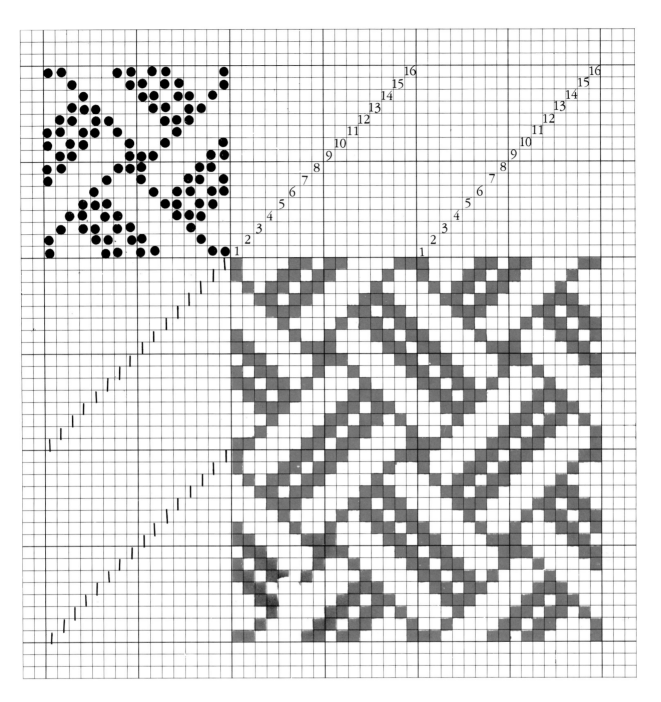

8-15a. Draft and diagram for figure 8-15.

8-16. Sixteen-harness twill by Gay McGeary. (Photo by Bernard Gordon)

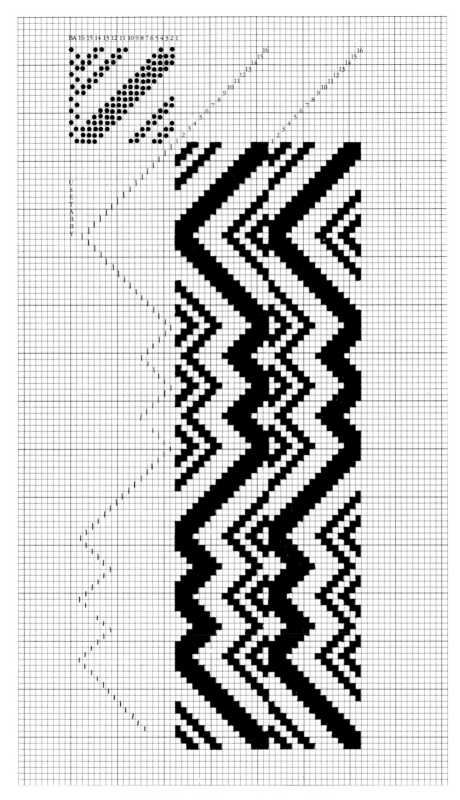

8-16a. Draft and diagram for figure 8-16.

8-17. Sixteen-harness design by Muriel Neeland. (Photo by Bernard Gordon)

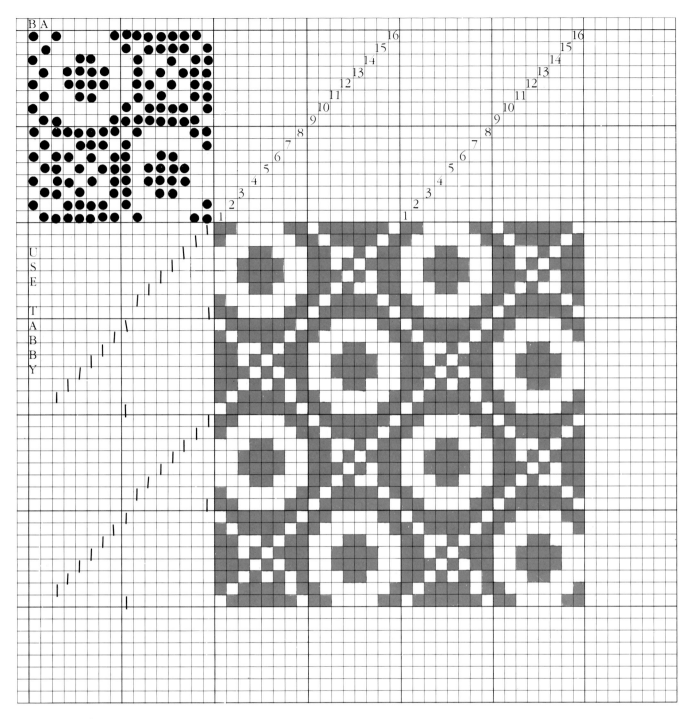

8-17a. Draft and diagram for figure 8-17.

8-18. Sixteen-harness design by Diane Fabeck. (Photo by Bernard Gordon)

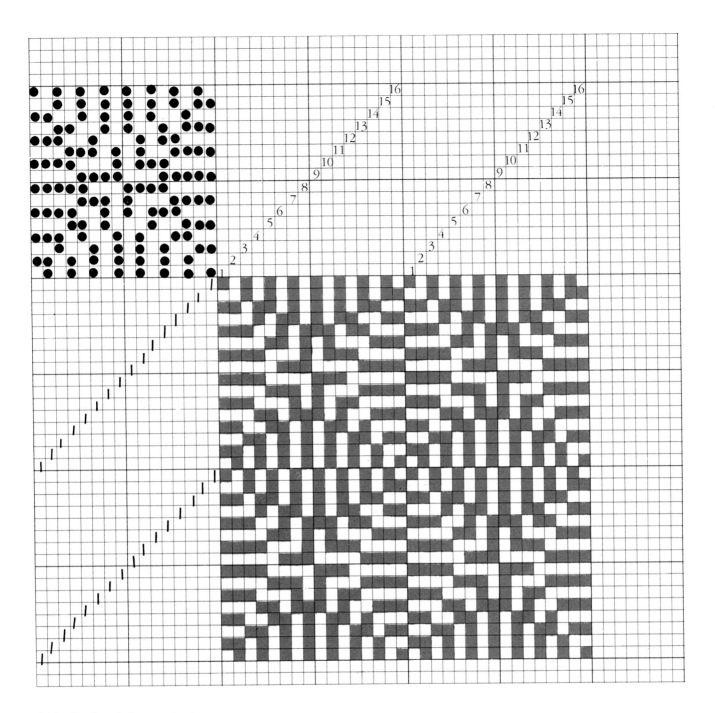

8-18a. Draft and diagram for figure 8-18.

8-19. Point twill bedcover, United States, ca. 1850. (Photo
courtesy of The Art Institute of Chicago)

162

The sixteen-harness bedcover in point twill composition shown in figure 8-19 is a rare example from the collection of The Art Institute of Chicago. Woven on a warp of natural cotton with weft of dark blue, light blue, orange, and brown wool, it includes several sections of different treadlings and equally handsome front and reverse sides.

8-19a. Partial draft for figure 8-19, by Judith Gordon.

8-20. *Passport,* by Jack Lenor Larsen; fabric in twill effect woven on Jacquard loom. (Photo courtesy of Jack Lenor Larsen)

8-21. *Wool Gathering*, by Janet Daniel; bedcover and hanging valance. (Photo courtesy of Janet Daniel)

9-1. Hanging in weft-faced twill blocks, by Mary Dinerstein
(Photo by George Suyeoka)

Chapter 9

Designs in Block Weaves

Fabric constructions may be based on allover patterns or on unit or block designs. Many structures, such as twills, plain weaves, lace weaves, and others, may be planned as blocks by repetition of their threading units. The profile draft (discussed in chapter 8) is the basis for the creation of such designs. It establishes the size of threading units for use with a variety of threading systems and shows the complete pattern in the weft proportions when completed in the drawdown or diagram. Proportions can be repeated evenly or can be varied in many ways by treadling the threaded blocks singly or in combinations. Arrangement of a simple block design on six harnesses is illustrated in figure 9-1. A twill is arranged in units of blocks, using the first three harnesses for the first block, and the second three

harnesses for the second block. Because the warp is widely spaced at 6 ends per inch, with two cotton threads doubled in heddles and reed, a weft-faced structure is created. The weft of natural, tan, taupe, and orange wool resulted in this attractive design.

Summer and Winter Weave

One of the most versatile block weaves is summer and winter, taking its name from the reversible colonial coverlets: dark on one side, light on the other. A characteristic of this weave, which can be made on four-harness as well as on multiple-harness looms, is the fact that a weft thread skips over no more than three warps, which makes this structure functional as well as decorative.

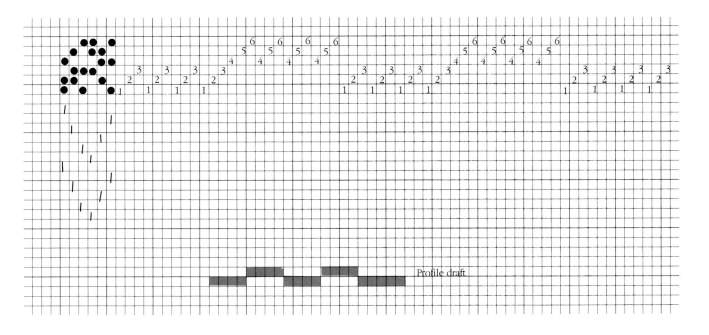

9-1a. Draft and profile for figure 9-1.

On four harnesses, 2 blocks are possible (fig.9-2a). Regular tie-down threads are usually placed on harnesses 1 and 2 alternating with a thread on a block harness. Unless the summer and winter is woven in weft-faced polychrome fashion, a tabby pick is included between each pattern shot. Tabbies in this weave structure are on harnesses 1-2 and 3-4. Figure 9-3, shows a simple two-block design, made interesting by changes in colors and direction. On a black cotton warp, threaded 5 double ends per inch, the weft colors in wool are:

Alternating white and light, 12 times. Alternating medium and dark, 12 times. Alternating white and light, 12 times.

White and off-white shades are used eight times as divisions. Since blocks and colors are used alternately, this piece is weft-faced, and no tabbies are needed. After weaving, the piece was turned horizontally so that the black warp ends of the beginning and end could be left hanging as decorations for the sides, and the end of the wool weft yarns were wrapped together for fringes. figure 9-3b, showing the extension of weft threads for fringe, illustrates the method.

Six blocks can be woven on eight harnesses (fig. 9-2b). The first and second harnesses, as before, are reserved for the tie-down threads, but the other six harnesses carry the blocks. Therefore, two blocks less than the number of available harnesses must always be planned for these weave structures. Tabby tie-ups are:

Tabby A, 1-2 Tabby B, 3-4-5-6-7-8.

Blocks may be tied up and treadled singly or in combinations, but one of the tie-down threads must always be raised together with desired pattern or block harnesses.

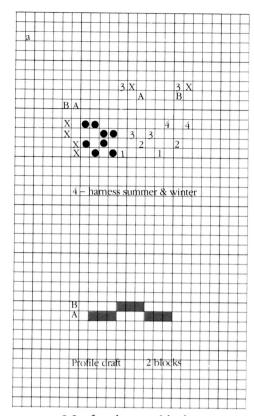

9-2a. four-harness blocks

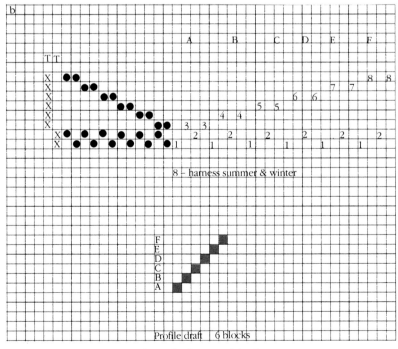

9-2b. eight-harness blocks

9-2. Drafts and profiles for summer and winter threadings

168

9-3. Hanging in polychrome summer and winter blocks, by
Mary Dinerstein. (Photo by Hector Garcia).

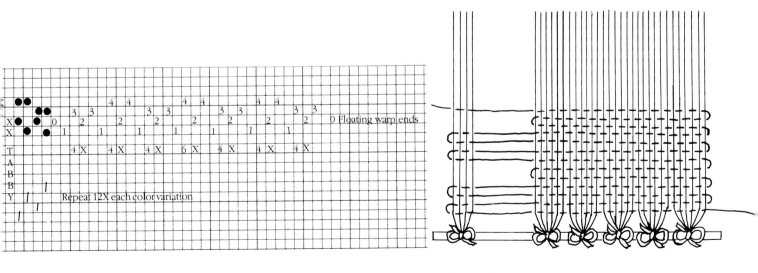

9-3a. Draft for figure 9-3.

9-3b. Weft fringe woven on the loom.
(Diagram by Irene Suyeoka)

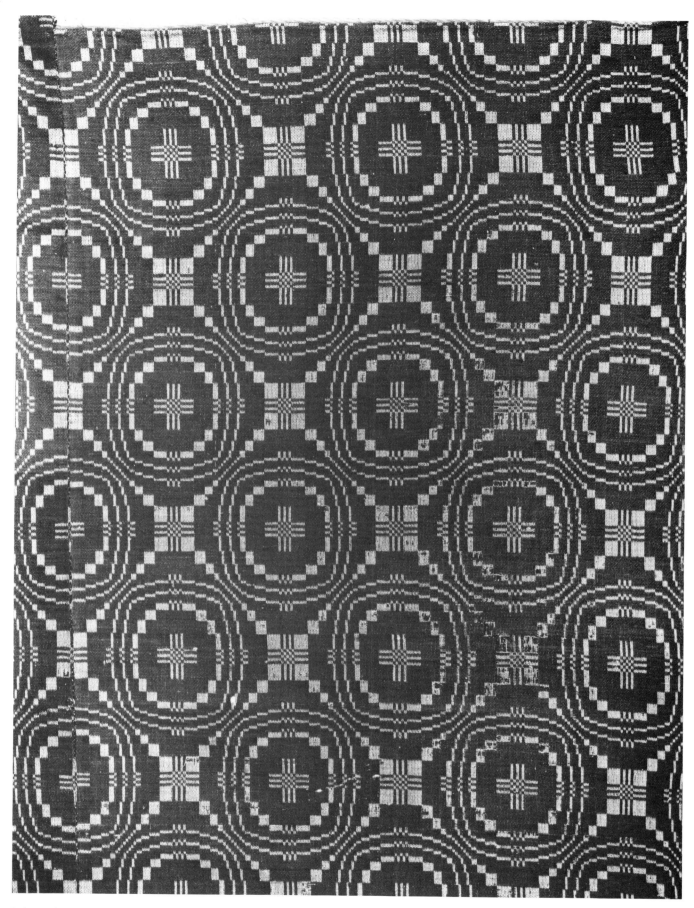

9-4. Bed cover in summer and winter technique; United States, 1820-25. (Photo courtesy of The Art Institute of Chicago)

9-5. Conversion and adaption of a tapestry (see figure 6-17) into summer and winter weave, by Barbara Gent. (Photo by George Suyeoka)

Flowers, Diamonds, and Stars, shown in figure 9-6, was inspired by colonial coverlet designs. By combining the single blocks shown in the profile drafts in different ways, Philis Alvic was able to incorporate many different designs in one hanging. This group of designs illustrates the variations possible with summer and winter weaves.

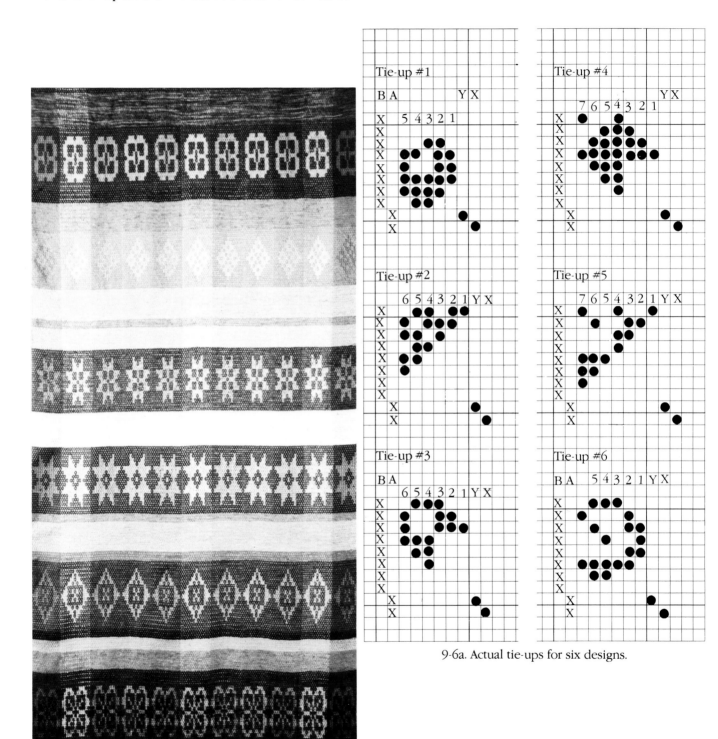

9-6a. Actual tie-ups for six designs.

9-6. *Flowers, Diamonds, and Stars,* by Philis Alvic; ten-harness summer and winter patterns. (Photo courtesy of Philis Alvic)

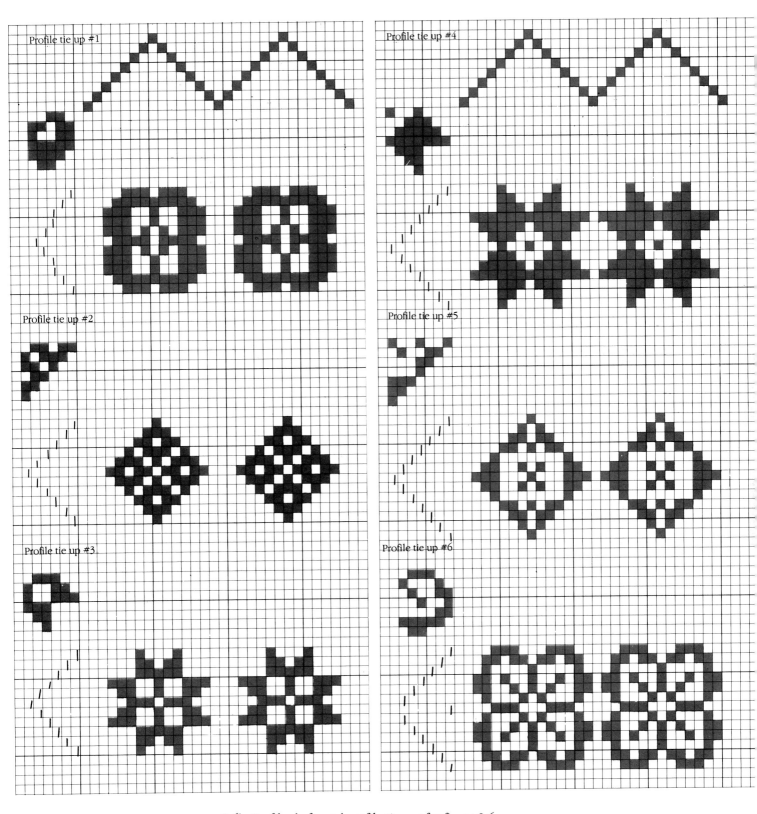

Profile tie up #1

Profile tie up #2

Profile tie up #3

Profile tie up #4

Profile tie up #5

Profile tie up #6

9-6b. Profile drafts and profile tie-ups for figure 9-6.

173

9-7. *Connecting Circles,* by Philis Alvic; twelve-harness summer and winter hanging shown sideways
(Photo courtesy of Philis Alvic)

Bergman Weave

This structure, called Bergman weave after its creator, converts the tie-down threads from two harnesses to three harnesses to create a background pattern. Draft 9-9a explains the threading principle. The pattern blocks may be varied by changing the block harnesses, but the tie-down progression must be consistent. As in summer and winter, one tie-down thread should always be raised with the desired block harness or harnesses. Philis Alvic applied this weave in her hanging *Indian Patterns* by a block arrangement of eight harnesses. The same artist wove *Sherbet Diamonds,* (fig. 9-9), which has seven pattern blocks.

9-8. *Indian Patterns,* by Philis Alvic; eight-harness Bergman weave. (Photo courtesy of Philis Alvic)

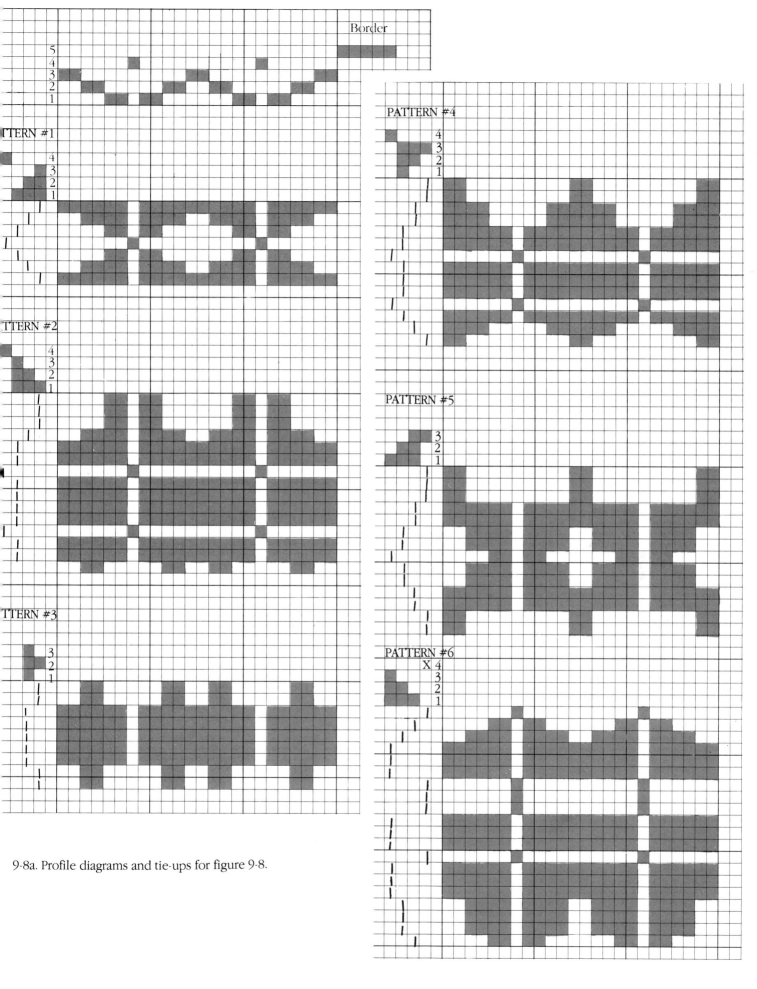

Border

PATTERN #1

PATTERN #2

PATTERN #3

PATTERN #4

PATTERN #5

PATTERN #6

9-8a. Profile diagrams and tie-ups for figure 9-8.

9-9. *Sherbet Diamonds,* by Philis Alvic; ten-harness Bergman weave. (Photo courtesy of Philis Alvic)

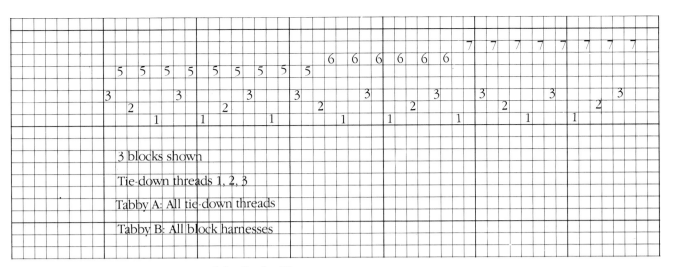

9-9a. Draft of Bergman weave structure.

3 blocks shown

Tie-down threads 1, 2, 3

Tabby A: All tie-down threads

Tabby B: All block harnesses

9-9b. Profile draft and tie-up for figure 9-9.

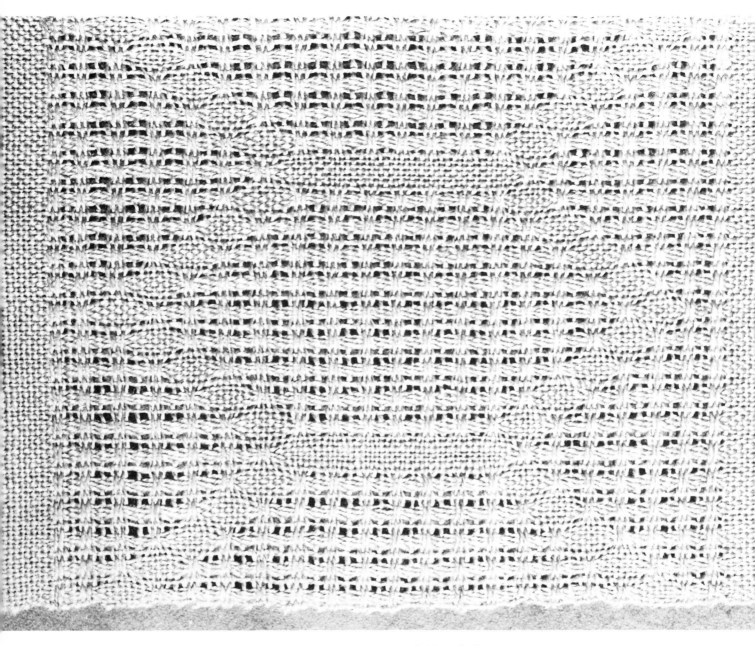

Lace Weaves

Two variations of loom-controlled lace are shown in figures 9-10 and 9-11. In Donna Masterson's example, figure 9-10, the diagram shows clearly that the lacy effect results from the arrangement of the tie-down threads in groups. The treadling follows a system that uses the same tabby several times in a row, opening up the spaces between groups of threads. She used 24 ends per inch with 20/2 linen warp and weft for her piece.

A different effect is achieved by using another tie-up. Mary Andrews wove her sample in Egyptian cotton, sett 30 ends per inch, for the geometric diamond blocks in figure 9-11.

9-10. Eight-harness Bronson lace weave by Donna Masterson. (Photo courtesy of Donna Masterson)

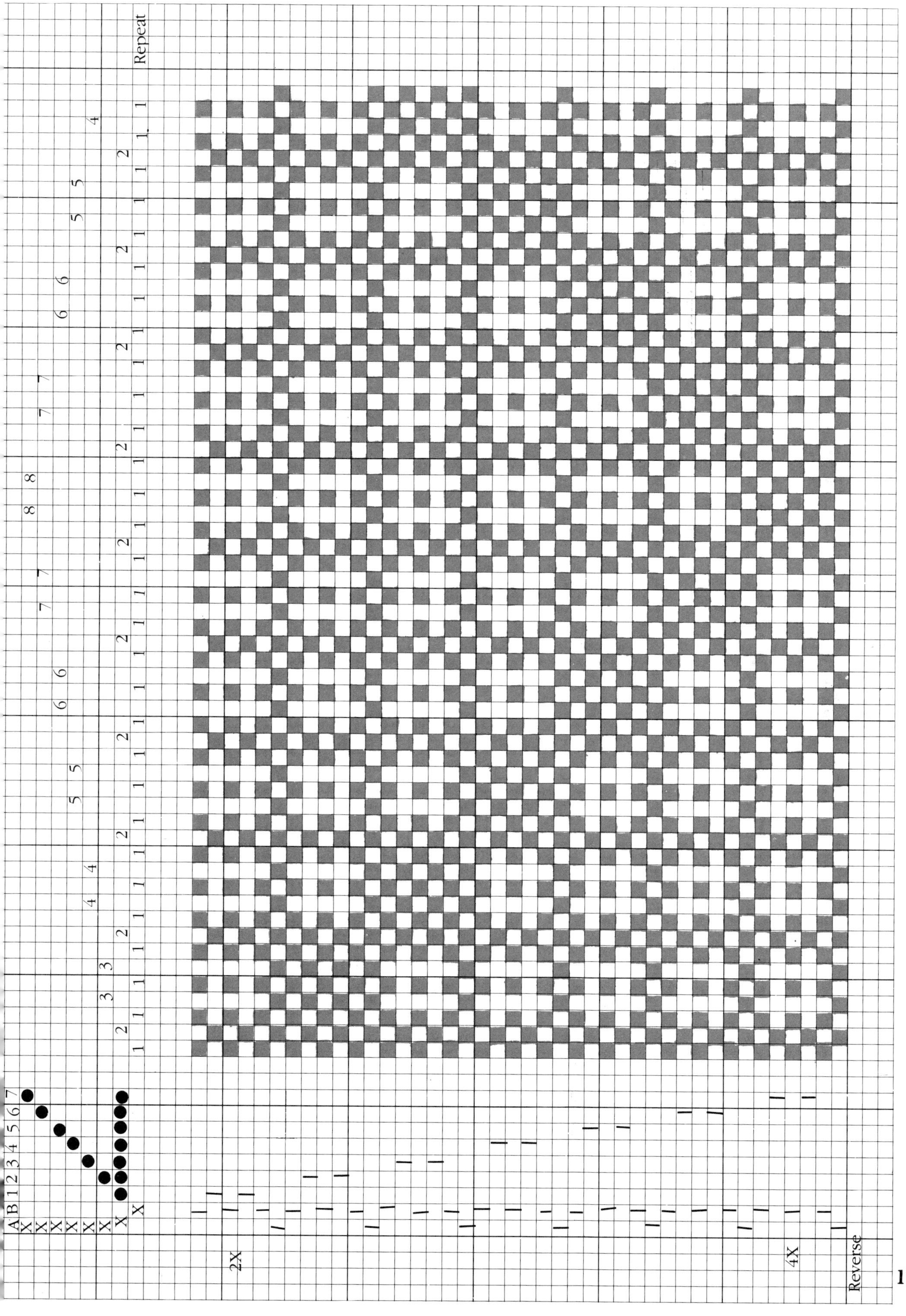

9-10a. Draft for figure 9-10, turned sideways.

9-11. Eight-harness lace by Mary Andrews. (Photo courtesy of Mary Andrews)

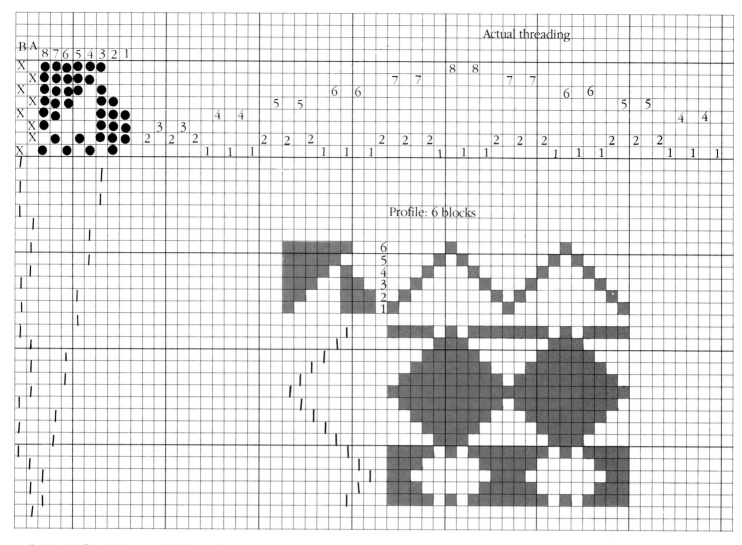

9-11a. Draft and diagram for figure 9-11.

Damask

The term *damask* was derived from the ancient city of Damascus in Syria, which by the twelfth century had become famous for its trade in elaborate and beautiful silks. Damask is a reversible block weave, most commonly made in a satin structure. The elegant designs are usually monochromatic and show up clearly in a warp satin on a weft satin background. The design can also be woven in weft satin, in which case the background must be a warp satin.

Satin structure needs a minimum of five harnesses. Although it is similar in appearance to a broken twill, no two points in the structure of the weave are connected. Two simple explanations of warp and weft satin for five and eight harnesses are illustrated in the drafts shown in figure 9-12.

The following method may be applied to construct a satin weave: a mathematical counter, also called a base, is used to find the interlacement points of warp and weft. This counter is found by separating the number of threads in the repeat (such as five-harness satin) into two parts. These two parts cannot be equal, cannot have number 1 as one of their components, must not have a common divisor with each other or with the total number, and must not be a multiple of each other. Therefore, an 8-end satin could be constructed with the help of counter 3 or 5, but not with 1, or 2 or 4, since these numbers divide evenly into 8. For a 5-end satin, a counter of either 2 or 3 can be used. A 9-end satin is possible with a counter of 2, 4, 5, or 7, but not with 3 or 6.

183

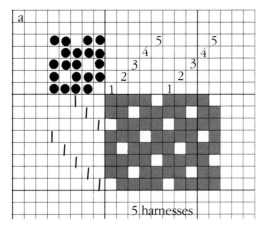

a. warp satin for five harnessess

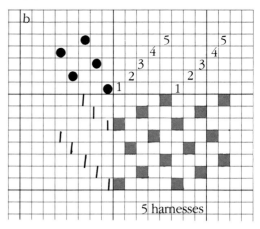

b. weft satin for five harnessess

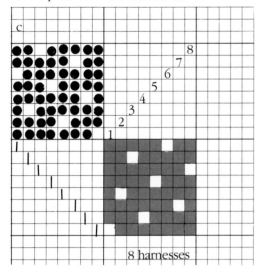

c. warp satin for eight harnessess

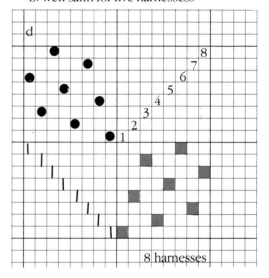

d. weft satin for eight harnessess.

9-12. Drafts for warp and weft satin weaves

Determining a correct counter is the first step in designing a satin weave. When the weave is drawn on graph paper, the first square in the lower left-hand corner is filled up, representing the first warp end to interlace with the first weft pick. For the next step, the counter number is added to number 1 (the first interlacing point) to determine the second pick. This method is continued until a repeat is reached, thus completing the weave construction. The formula can be written out in an easily understandable fashion. For a 5-end satin (which makes the number 5 the limit of the repeat), using counter 2:

    1 plus 2 is 3
    3 plus 2 is 5
    5 plus 2 is 7; minus 5 is 2
    2 plus 2 is 4
    4 plus 2 is 6; minus 5 is 1

With the arrival at number 1, the repeat is established. The sequence of picks (1, 3, 5, 2, 4) repeats itself.

For two blocks, woven as patterns side by side, a minimum of ten harnesses is needed. If a multi-harness loom is not available, broken twills are sometimes substituted for similar effects and the structure is referred to as *false damask*.

Pat Kinsella used a satin weave as ground for the patterns, which were picked up by hand, in *Tessera* (fig. 9-13). The weft is fine sewing thread with four threads of different colors wound together to form one weft element. In another example, figure 9-15, a fifteen harness damask in three blocks uses an interesting profile draft for an exceptionally beautiful sample.

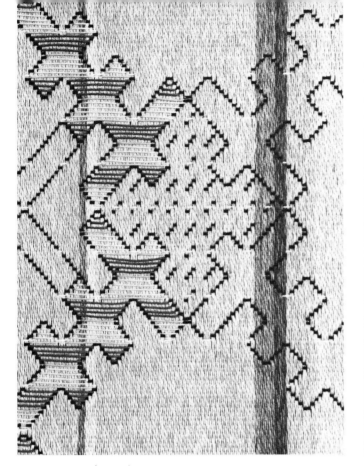

9-13. *Tessera,* (detail) by Pat Kinsella; damask weave. (Photo courtesy of Pat Kinsella)

9-14. Twenty-harness damask by Antonia Kormos. (Photo by Bernard Gordon)

9-13a. *GYRE* (detail) by Pat Kinsella. (Photo courtesy of Pat Kinsella)

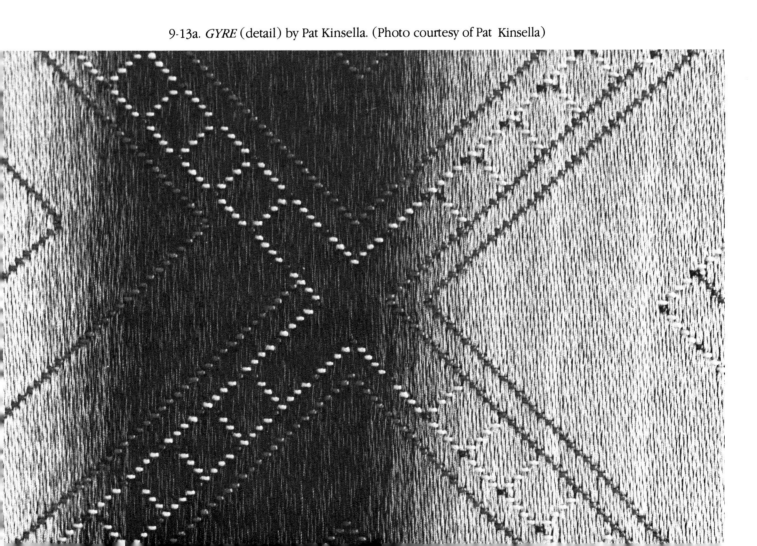

9-15. Fifteen-harness damask by Charleen Arnold. (Photo by Bernard Gordon)

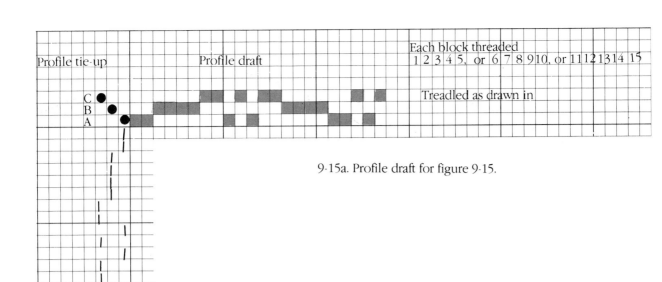

Profile tie-up   Profile draft   Each block threaded
1 2 3 4 5, or 6 7 8 9 10, or 11 12 13 14 15

Treadled as drawn in

9-15a. Profile draft for figure 9-15.

Supplementary Warp

Many geometric designs are made with the use of a supplementary warp. The function of such a warp is decoration, and it is called "supplementary" because it is a nonessential addition to a ground weave that would be complete without it. A supplementary element can also be an extra decorative weft thread. Designing with a supplementary warp is just like designing block weaves by themselves, with harness 1 and 2 forming the plain weave ground fabric. Since the supplementary warp is usually heavier than or of a different sett from the ground warp, two tensions are needed. If a second warp beam is not available, the supplementary warp can hang in chains over the back beam. The method shown here is loom-controlled. On 8 harnesses, 6 pattern blocks are possible. One tie-down thread must always be used together with one block harness or a combination of block harnesses.

A most intriguing use of supplementary warp can be seen in the apron shown in figure 9-16. Woven on a complex loom, it was originally threaded on 14 harnesses. The tie-up was then transferred to the mechanical device of the loom. In order to weave a handloom version, Judith Gordon designed, drafted, and wove an eight-harness adaptation of the apron pattern (fig. 9-17). Figures 9-18 and 9-19 show the same threading draft with different tie-ups and treadlings used to create each of the individual designs. Woven on the same warp, the background is 10/2 cotton, 24 ends per inch, and the supplementary warp is the same size in wool. Two ends of cotton and two ends of wool were sleyed together in each dent of a 12-dent reed.

9-16. Wool apron with supplementary warp design, from Finland. (Photo by Hector Garcia)

187

9-17. Adaptation of apron design for eight harnes
by Judith Gordon. (Photo by Bernard Gordon.

9-17a. Draft and diagrams by Judith Gordon.

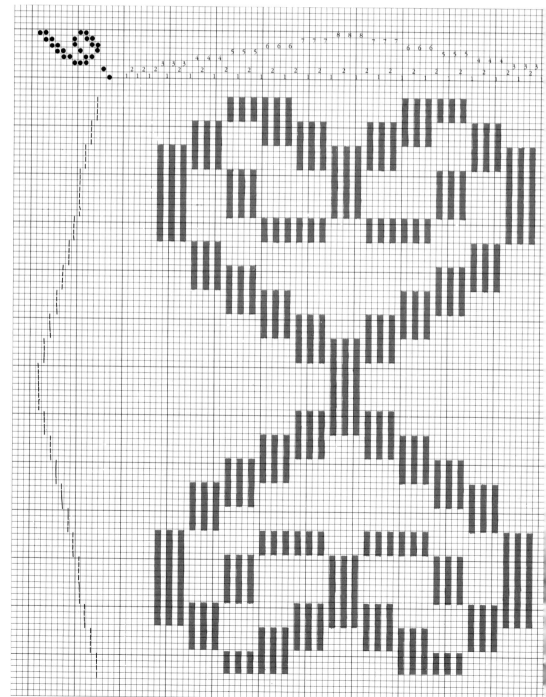

188

9-18. Design with supplementary warp, by Judith Gordon. (Photo by Bernard Gordon)

9-18a. Draft and diagram for figure 9-18.

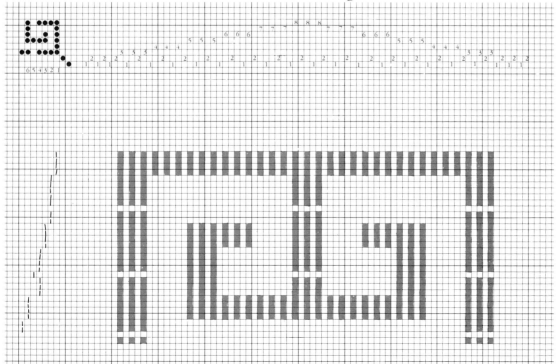

9-19. Variation of supplementary warp design, by Judith Gordon. (Photo by Bernard Gordon)

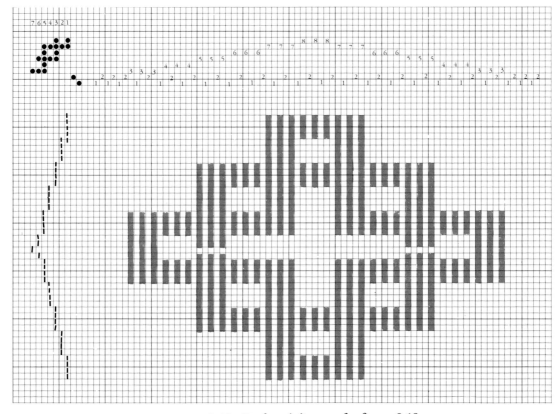

9-19a. Draft and diagram for figure 9-19.

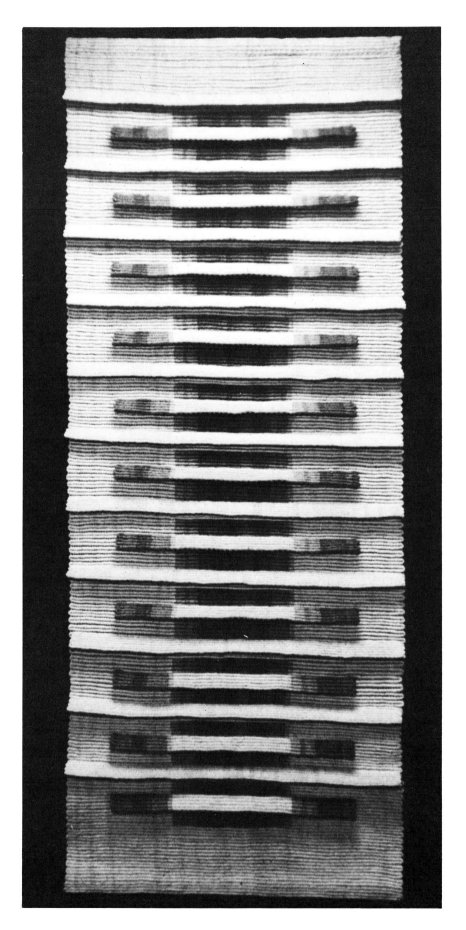

9-20. Hanging with supplementary warp by Michi Ouchi.

9-21. *On the Shoulders of the Mountain,* by Margaret Windeknecht; stuffer rug. (Photo courtesy of Margaret Windeknecht)

Stuffer Rug

The stuffer rug has double-woven surfaces and is therefore completely reversible. It is most effective when woven in strong geometric designs and definite light and dark color contrasts. The unique feature of the stuffer rug lies in the addition of an extra set of warp threads between 2 layers of weaving warp and weft. This stuffer warp makes the rug very thick and durable but is hidden between the top and reverse surfaces of the rug. Only the weaving warp shows on the surfaces, interweaving with the weft.

Although the geometric design in figure 9-21 is planned in the same block system as summer and winter, this technique involves two warps, as illustrated in figure 7-14. The stuffer warp is hidden between the layers of surfaces and controls the block design. The weaving warp, threaded on harnesses 1 and 2, shows up in plain weave in front and back. It takes up more yardage than the stuffer, has fewer threads per inch, and is woven at a different tension. Unless two warp beams are available, the weaving warp hangs in chains over the back beam (fig. 7-14a and b). When two warp beams are available, the stuffer warp is wound on one beam and the weaving warp on the other beam. The sett of the stuffer warp is 20 or 24 ends per inch. There are always four stuffer warps between two weaving warps. Each weaving warp must be in a dent by itself, but depending on the choice of the sett and the reed, the four stuffer warps can be placed either in one dent together or threaded in two adjacent dents (fig. 9-21b).

Two contrasting colors are needed in the weft to create the design. In the tie-up, block harnesses can be used singly or in any desired combination.

Each row of design consists of four picks: For a solid color, the treadling sequence is:

    1—weave color A
    1 (plus all block harnesses)—weave color B
    2—weave color A
    2 (plus all block harnesses)—weave color B

For the pattern, the sequence is:

    1 (plus desired block harnesses)—weave color A
    1 (plus opposite block harnesses)—weave color B
    2 (plus desired block harnesses)—weave color A
    2 (plus opposite block harnesses)—weave color B

Repeat these four picks as often as needed to build up the design. This technique was originally developed by Mary M. Atwater and is described in *The Art of Weaving* chapter 9.

The profile draft shows the arrangement of the blocks, and the tie-ups in numbers show which harnesses are raised for pattern and background (9-21a).

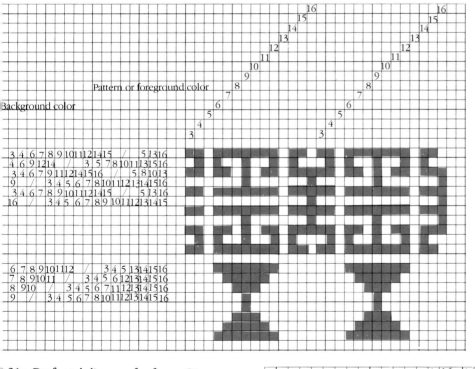

9-21a. Draft and diagram for figure 21.

9-21b. Threading system for stuffer rug technique.

1 and 2 = weaving warp

11 = 2 stuffer warps in same heddle

10-1. Bed cover in double weave, attributed to John Landes, about 1820-30. (Photo courtesy of The Art Institute of Chicago)

Chapter 10

Designs in Loom-controlled Double Weaves

In contrast to the pick-up double weave discussed in chapter 7, loom-controlled double weave geometric blocks may be threaded directly into the harnesses. As in all patterned double weaves, the two layers must be in contrasting colors, making a positive and negative side of pattern and ground. Twice as many warp threads as needed for one layer must be planned.

On four harnesses, only one block is possible because each plain weave layer needs two harnesses (fig. 10-2). To weave the top layer, half of the top layer threads are raised. For the bottom layer, both the complete top layer and the first half of the bottom layer are raised. For the third pick, the second half of the top layer is raised and for the fourth pick the complete top layer plus the second half of the bottom layer are raised.

Two blocks can be threaded on eight harnesses; three blocks on twelve harnesses; and on sixteen harnesses, four blocks are possible. Top and bottom layers are woven alternately. At the same time as the first pick of the first block is woven, the desired threads from the second, third, or fourth blocks are raised in the tie-up to make the pattern. This system continues until the rotation of the two layers is finished. The draft in figure 10-3 shows the system of arranging two blocks in black and white for two different layers on eight harnesses.

Once the weaver understands this basic principle of double weave, the more complicated patterns can be attempted. Each block must be woven in a rotation of four treadles in order to weave top and bottom every time. All harnesses used in one pick across the width of

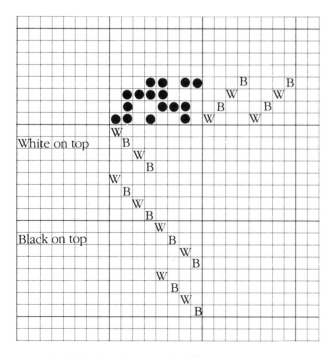

10-2. Draft for four-harness double weave.

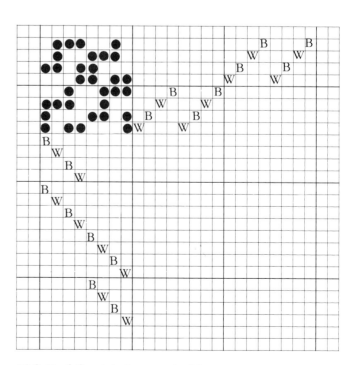

10-3. Draft for eight-harness double weave.

the warp, must be tied up to one treadle. Since multi-harness patterns need many treadles and tie-up combinations, the diagrams (draw-downs) are usually presented in profile drafts, indicating the blocks in the threading and the blocks that are woven together. The length of each block in Ruth Holroyd's sixteen-harness double weave (fig. 10-4), for example, is shown in the profile draft (fig. 10-4a), but the actual tie-up is also added for clarification. Each block is threaded in a straight twill and repeated according to the profile draft. Four colors—yellow and orange in one block, red and orange in the second block, red and natural in the third block, and yellow and natural in the fourth block—always in alternating light and dark colors in the heddles, are used.

10-4. Sixteen-harness double weave by Ruth N. Holroyd. (Photo by Bernard Gordon)

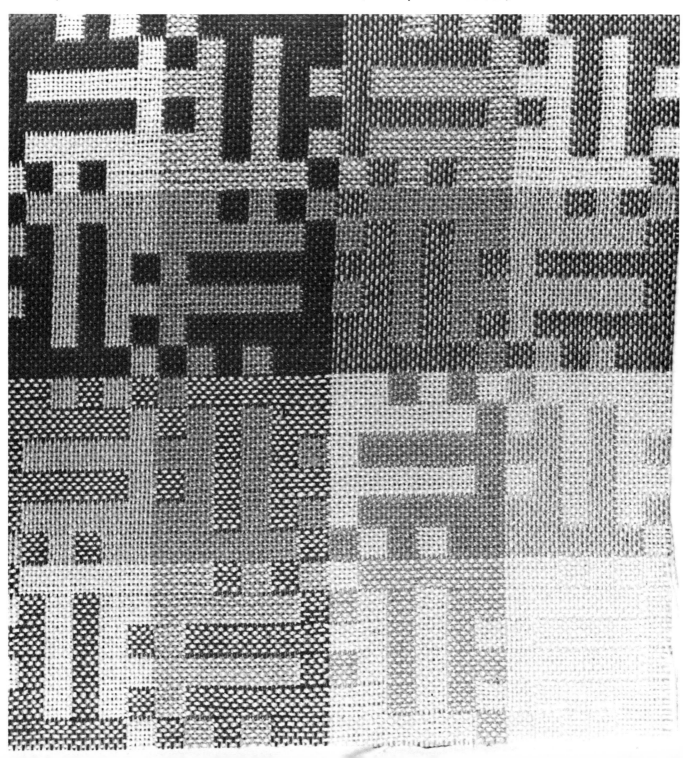

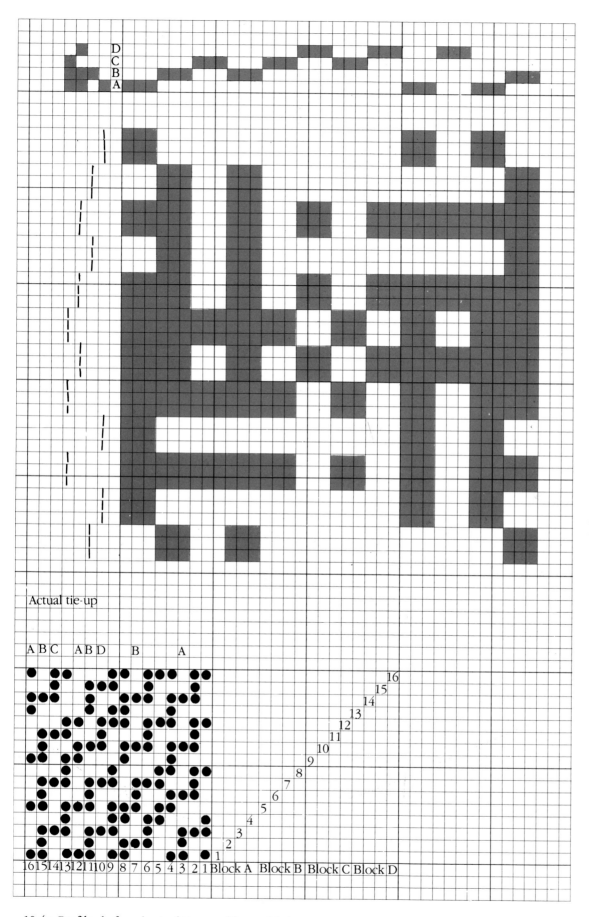

10-4a. Profile draft and actual tie-up of figure 10-4.

The same idea and draft can be used for the creation of individual color schemes and pattern changes and presents challenging problems for the weaver using a multi-harness loom.

Contemporary weavers are often inspired by traditional coverlet patterns (fig. 10-5) and weave their own inter pretations. Marian Hoskinson, for example, used a 20/2 cotton warp in alternating orange and rust colors, sett 60 ends per inch in a 15 dent reed; the profile draft and draw-down as well as the actual tie-up for sixteen harnesses are illustrated in figure 10-5a. As in all double weaves, the fabric is reversible and could be successfully woven in heavier yarns and larger patterns for a variety of functional projects.

10-5. Sixteen-harness double weave by Marian K. Hoskinson. (Photo by Bernard Gordon)

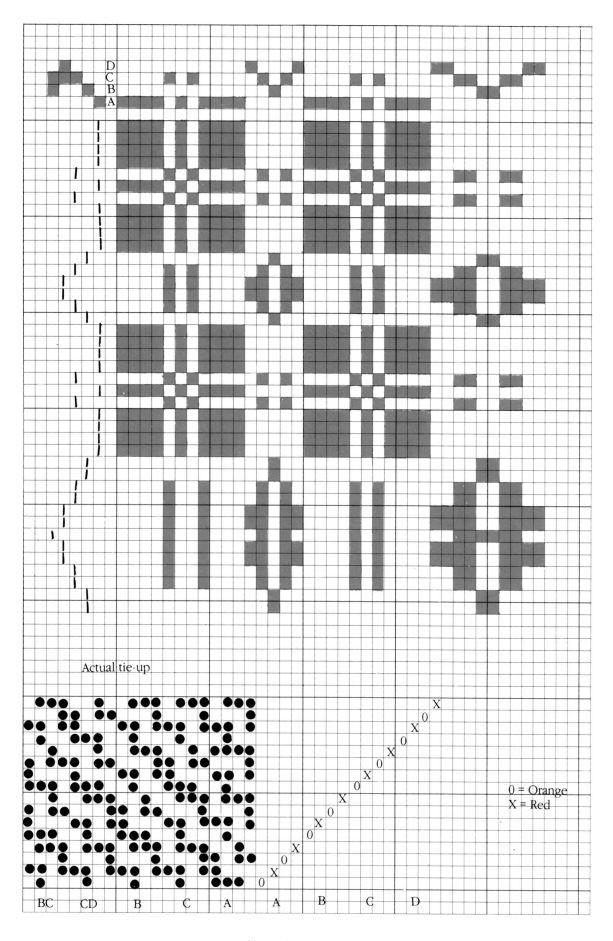

10-5a. Profile draft and actual tie-up for figure 10-5.

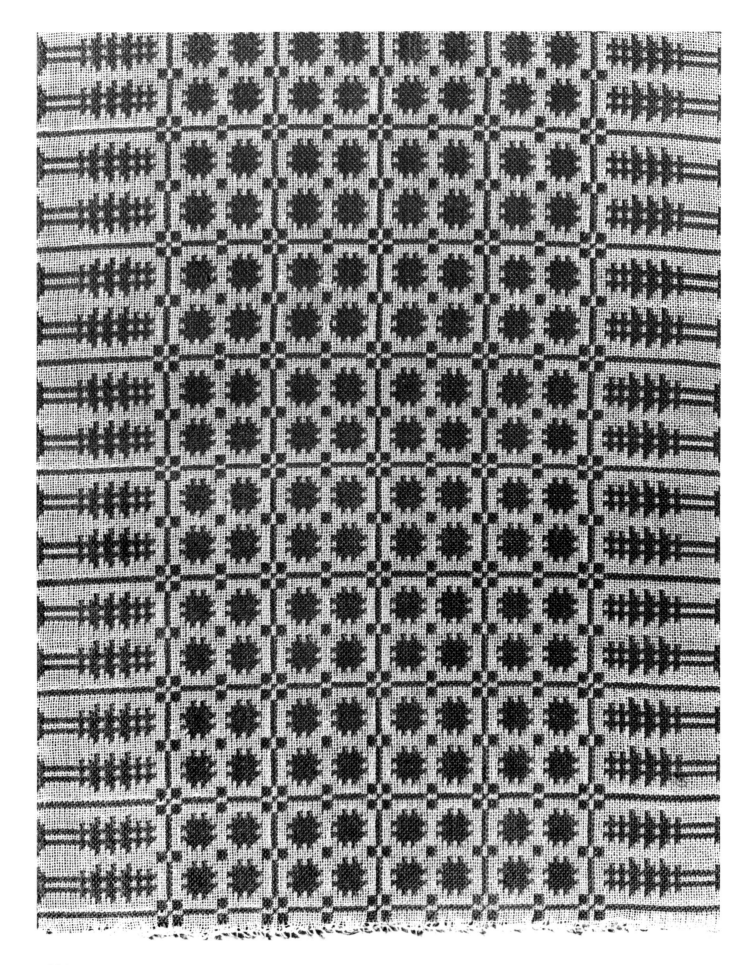

200

To add another dimension to the project of design, coupled with the challenge of technique, the complicated four-block double weave by Muriel M. Neeland (fig. 10-6) was re-created by Judith Gordon in a six-harness summer and winter draft (fig. 10-7).

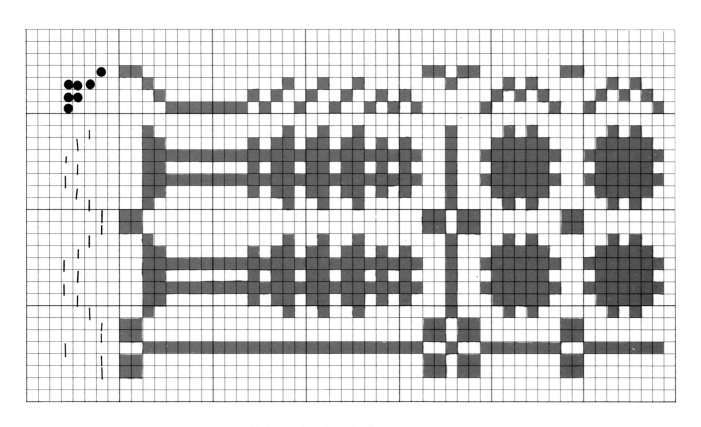

10-6a. Profile draft for figure 10-6.

10-6. Four-block double weave on sixteen-harnessess, by Muriel M. Neeland. (Photo by Bernard Gordon)

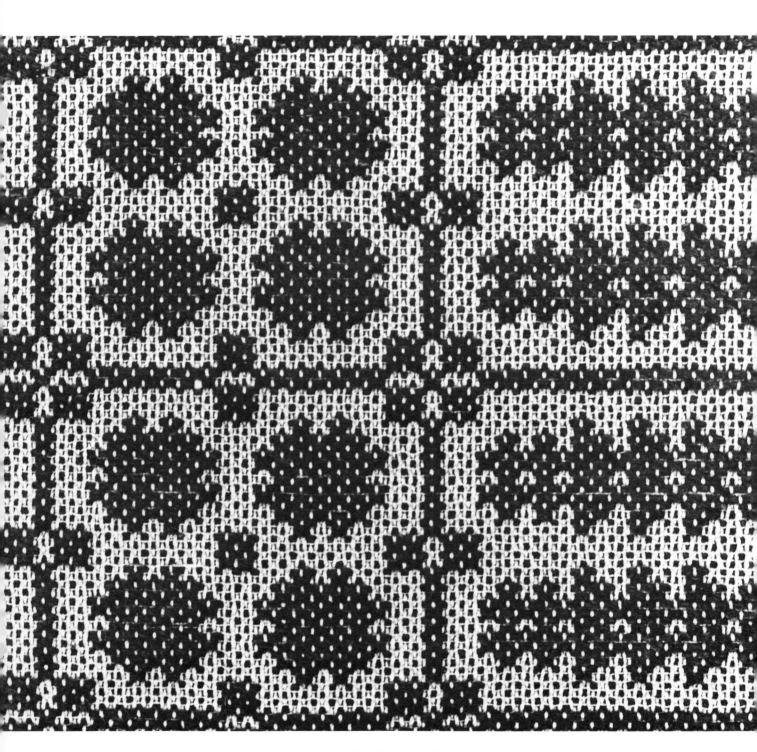

10-7. Conversion of a four-block double weave design to a six-harness summer and winter weave, by Judith Gordon. (Photo by Bernard Gordon)

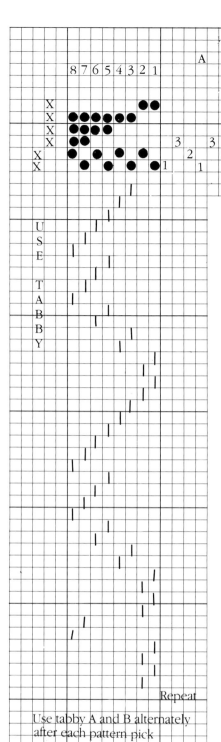

10-7a. Draft for figure 10-7.

U
S
E

T
A
B
B
Y

Repeat

Use tabby A and B alternately after each pattern pick

8 7 6 5 4 3 2 1   A   B   C   D

Rudolph Fuchs considered it a challenge to design a double weave on sixteen-harnesses in a plain and twill combination (fig. 10-8). Using two white and two tan cotton threads sleyed together in an 8-dent reed, he succeeded in weaving a distinctive design with a diamond twill within a square, and plain weave color squares on white background.

10-8. Double weave with diamond design, by Rudolph Fuchs. (Photo by Bernard Gordon)

10-9. Double weave on sixteen-harnesses, by Isabel Abel. (Photo by Bernard Gordon)

10-10. Reverse side of figure 10-9.

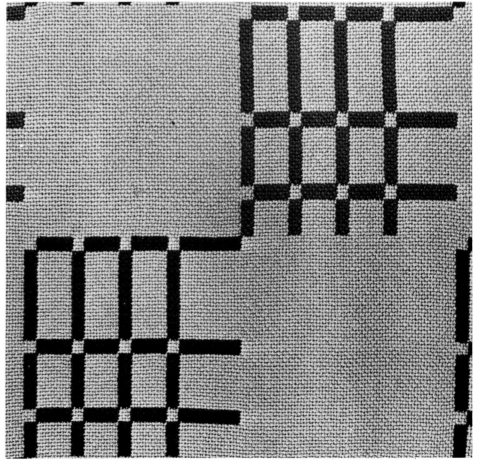

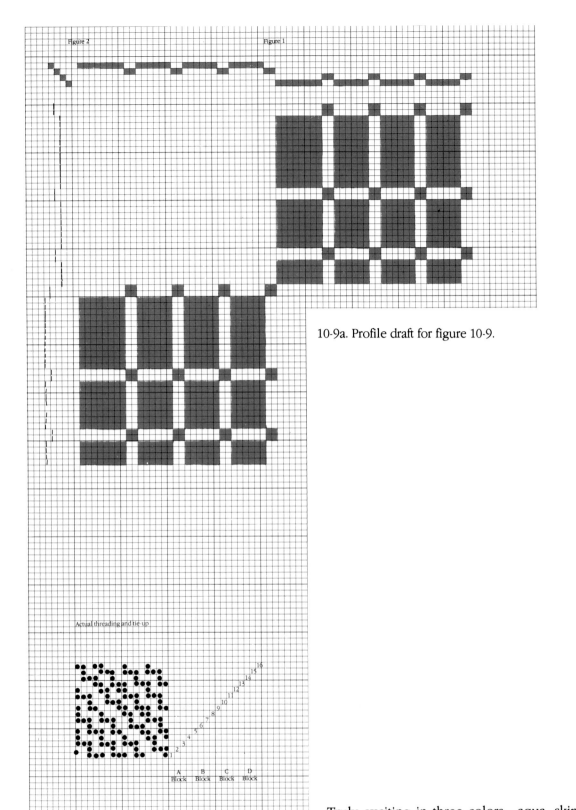

10-9a. Profile draft for figure 10-9.

Truly exciting in three colors—aqua, skipper blue, and red—is Isabel Abel's sample of a strong square and rectangular design (fig. 10-9). Sett 48 ends per inch in pearl cotton yarns, the aqua background color was threaded on harnesses 1, 3, 5, 7, 9, 11, 13, 15 all the way through, while blue was threaded on harnesses 2, 4, 6, 8 in one block, and red on harnesses 10, 12, 14, 16 on the other block. Therefore, one section is woven in aqua and blue warp and weft, the other in aqua and red warp and weft.

10-11. Multi-colored double weave by Diane Fabeck. (Photo by Bernard Gordon)

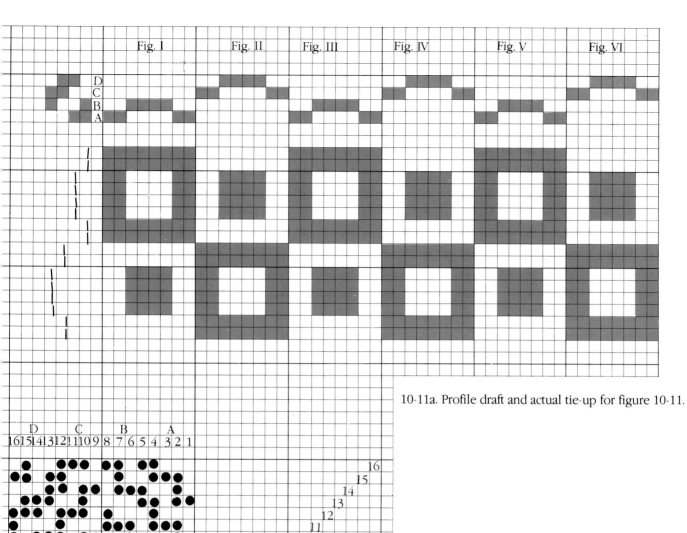

Fig. I   Fig. II   Fig. III   Fig. IV   Fig. V   Fig. VI

10-11a. Profile draft and actual tie-up for figure 10-11.

Using colors of many shades and values, Diane Fabeck achieved great interest in a design of squares within squares (fig. 10-11). Her colors in 20/2 wool, sett 40 ends per inch in a 10-dent reed, consist of green, violet, and turquoise in warp and weft. By using the colors alternately, sometimes green and sometimes turquoise and violet, and sometimes green and violet, in many modifications, she was able to produce amazing variations of tones and shades. The profile draft, draw down and actual tie-up are shown in fig. 10-11a.

207

Of *Concept* by Richard Landis, which is shown in figure 10-12, Jack Lenor Larsen says: "Basically it is a tonal system composed of fifty-two brilliant polychromatic shades, juxtaposed to a ground of muted bronze. The reverse side employs the same colors for what may be the world's most complex plaid fabric".

10-12. *Concept,* by Richard Landis; polychrome design. (Photo courtesy of Jack Lenor Larsen)

Variations

Loom-woven , but with a touch of the weaver's hand, are two hangings by Eunice Anders (fig. 10-13). These eight-harness double weaves were woven in bands, with the top and bottom layers interchanging at various intervals. Each band was woven with its own small shuttle. The underlayer shows through the open spaces in areas designed in advance. After the hanging was removed from the loom, the two sides of the individual bands were pulled up and pinched together with paper clips; the artist then decided which lines and effects interpreted her design and ideas. For the final result, each intersection was sewn together with invisible thread.

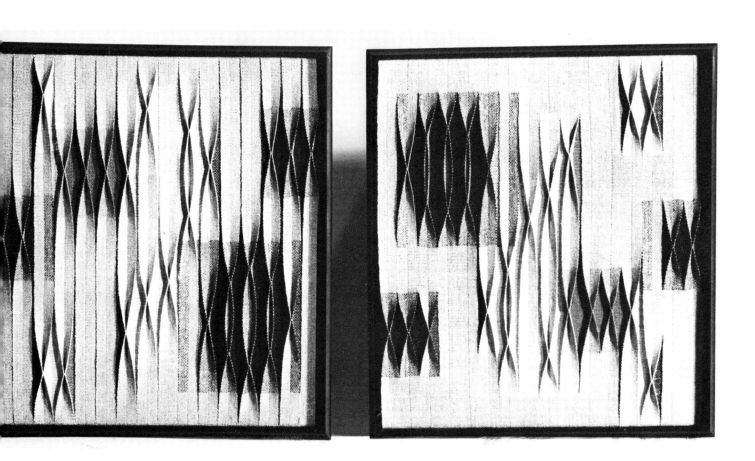

10-13. *Navajo I and II,* by Eunice B. Anders; framed double weave. (Photo courtesy of Eunice B. Anders)

The small sculptures shown in figure 10-14 were woven in geometric forms by the same artist. The warp was 6 ends per inch per layer in cotton seine twine, and the weft a Finnish linen yarn. The weft-faced structures were beaten very hard and therefore needed no stiffening. In some of the pieces, the layers were intersected in the center by taking the shuttle out of the warp and completing the rotation as shown in figure 10-15.

Whether weaver-controlled or loom-controlled, double weaves are most satisfactory methods for executing simple or complex geometric designs.

10-14. *Intersecting Planes Progression,* by Eunice B. Anders. (Photo courtesy of Eunice B. Anders)

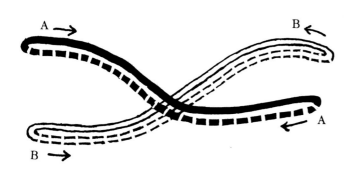

10-15. Interchanging layers in the center.

Conclusion

I realize that many of the techniques in which geometric designs are presented in this book may, at first sight be awe-inspiring, if not overwhelming. For this reason, the reader must understand that each technique is a study by itself and is presented as a possibility for transforming a design idea into a realistically woven fabric. My intent is to stimulate the weaver not only to create a good design, but also to explore many techniques for its successful execution. If each chapter is approached in this fashion, it will become obvious that geometric designs are very exciting and versatile, no matter what final form may be selected by the weaver. The square, the rectangle, and the circle, all acquire a life of their own and a characteristic based on the technique in which they are executed.

Just as each artist included here has expressed ideas and conceptions, so should the reader find joy and satisfaction in solving his or her own geometric ideas creatively on the loom.

10-16. Variation of small woven structures, by Irene Suyeoka.
(Photo courtesy of Irene Suyeoka)

A-1. Rug sample with cutup yarns, by Irene Suyeoka. (Photo courtesy of Irene Suyeoka)

Appendix: Study Problems

Study Problems

Just as study groups are valuable stimuli for exploration and experimentation, so guidelines are valuable for following up ideas that may have been stimulated by reading this book. Many times, a weaver on his or her own needs a given task in order to find the way out of a labyrinth of multitudinous possibilities that, while exciting and stimulating in themselves, actually present concrete and systematic challenges for study.

The following problems, based on this book, are meant to be helpful to weavers who may wish to assemble a valuable collection of their own geometric designs.

Problem 1

Design a rug using proportions and space divisions of dynamic symmetry.
a. Draw the outline of a rectangle according to proportions and measurements of dynamic symmetry.
b. Draw diagonal, vertical, and/or horizontal lines within the rectangle to determine divisions of areas. When you are satisfied with these divisions, make a copy of the skeleton design.
c. In this copy fill in spaces in black and white.
d. In another copy of the same rectangle fill in spaces in color blends.
e. In another copy of the same rectangle fill in spaces with cut-up yarn pasted to the background to see the design in the texture of a woven rug (fig. A-1).

Problem 2

Use the method of tessellation to design a tile pattern from a basic shape.
a. Draw a small geometric shape and use one mirror to create reversed image designs.
b. Use several mirrors to create different variations of the same shape.

Problem 3

Create four geometric collages.
a. Using dark cut-out paper on a light background, arrange two shapes so that patterns and backgrounds are interchangeable.
b. Cut out and arrange three or more different shapes on a background to make a pleasing balanced design.
c. Arrange various cutout shapes on a paper background and include textures such as strings, yarns, and so on, for a more intricate design.
d. Create another design of various shapes in light, medium, and dark values, achieving the illusion of transparency.

Problem 4

Make three collages in geometric designs.
a. Draw outlines of three geometric shapes on paper within a perimeter.
b. Fill in spaces in black and white.
c. Fill in spaces in textured materials, such as shredded paper, corrugated paper, cork, pebbles, rice, peas, and so on. Use a thin layer of glue to hold textures in place.

Problem 5

Make three collages with dried leaves.
a. Arrange leaves on plain white or natural background.
b. Arrange leaves, using various colored paper as background.
c. Arrange leaves and include cutout shapes in colored paper in the design.

Problem 6

Choose your favorite design and weave it in one or several techniques, (use only black and white yarns in order to test the strength of the design).

a. Weave a sample in tapestry techniques.
b. Weave a sample in pile techniques.
c. Weave a sample in the pick-up double weave technique.
d. Observe the effect and the influence of techniques on the clarity of outlines and shapes.

Problem 7

Explore one or more techniques presented in this book that you have not tried before.

a. Weave a sample using overshot in various treadlings.
b. Weave a sample using overshot in star and in rose fashion.
c. Weave a sample using name draft or alphabet weaving in overshot or twill.

Problem 8

Explore double weave techniques for geometric shapes.

a. Weave a sample in weaver-controlled pick-up technique.
b. Weave a sample using loom-controlled double weaves in tubular designs with stuffed areas.
c. Weave a sample using loom-controlled double weaves in block or pattern designs.
d. Explore and observe the influence of colors in emphasizing or obstructing clarity of designs.

Problem 9

Explore and weave various shapes, analyze structures and find the most suitable techniques for weaving individual shapes. Adapt and weave samples of the following:

a. Diamond shapes (twills, pattern weaves, and so on).
b. Triangles (soumak weaves, pile, tapestry, double weaves).
c. Squares and rectangles (block weaves, loom-controlled double weaves and so on).

Problem 10

Design a project in geometric shapes for any of the techniques you have explored.

a. Decide on yarns, setts, threadings, and structures.
b. Weave a small prototype for the planned project, such as wall hanging, rug, or fabric.
c. Use this prototype to weave a finished piece.

Glossary

Of Geometric Terms

Circle: a line every point of which is equally distant from a point within which is called the center.

Circumference: the perimeter of a circle; the external boundary of a figure or object.

Cone: a solid with a flat, round base that tapers evenly to a point at the top.

Cube: the regular solid of six equal square sides.

Cylinder: the surface traced by a straight line moving parallel to a fixed straight line and intersecting a fixed curve.

Decagon: a plane polygon of ten angles and ten sides.

Decahedron: a solid figure having ten flat, sharp-angled surfaces.

Diagonal: a straight line or plane that cuts across in a slanting direction, often from corner to corner.

Diameter: the length of a straight line through the center of an object.

Diamond: a square- or rhombus-shaped configuration usually having a distinctive orientation.

Geometric: utilizing rectilinear or simple curvilinear motifs or outlines in design.

Graph: symbolic diagram using a grid.

Grid: a network of uniformly spaced horizontal and perpendicular lines.

Hedron: geometricular figure having a specified form or number of surfaces.

Heptagon: a polygon of seven angles and seven sides.

Hexagon: a polygon of six angles and six sides.

Hexagram: a figure formed by completing externally an equilateral triangle on each side of a regular hexagon.

Hexahedron: a polyhedron of six faces.

Icosahedron: a polyhedron of twenty faces.

Module: a standard or unit of measurement.

Octagon: a polygon of eight angles and eight sides.

Octahedron: a solid bounded by eight plane faces.

Ogee: a pointed arch having on each side a reversed curve near the apex.

Oval: having the shape of an egg.

Parallel: lines extending in the same direction, everywhere equidistant and never meeting.

Parallelogram: a quadrilateral with opposite sides parallel and equal.

Pentagon: a polygon of five angles and five sides.

Pentahedron: a solid bounded by five faces.

Perimeter: the boundary of a closed plane figure.

Plane: a flat or level surface.

Poly: many.

Polygon: a closed plane figure bounded by straight lines.

Polyhedron: a solid formed by plane faces.

Proportion: the relation of one part to another or to the whole with respect to magnitude, quantity, or degree.

Quadrilateral: having four sides.

Ratio: the relationship in quantity, amount, or size between two or more things; proportion.

Rectangle: a parallelogram in which all angles are right angles.

Rhomboid: a parallelogram in which the angles are oblique and adjacent sides are unequal.

Rhombus: an equilateral parallelogram usually having oblique angles.

Root: a number that, when multiplied by itself an indicated number of times, gives a specified number: the square root of sixteen is four because four times four equals sixteen.

Sphere: a globular body; ball.

Spheroid: a figure resembling a sphere.

Square: a rectangle having four equal sides.

Square Root: see Root.

Star: a conventional figure with five or more points that represents a star.

Symmetry: correspondence in size, shape, and relative position of parts on opposite sides of a dividing line or medial plane, or about a center or axis; balanced proportion.

Tessellation: a careful juxtaposition of elements into a coherent pattern.

Tetrahedron: a polyhedron of four faces.

Triangle: a polygon having three sides.

Bibliography

Design

Boas, Franz. *Primitive Art.* New York: Dover Publications, Inc., 1955.

Collins, Henry B.; DeLaguma, Frederick; Carpenter, Edmund; and Stone, Peter. *2000 Years of American Eskimo and Indian Art.* Washington, DC: National Gallery of Art, 1973.

Dye, Daniel Sheets. *Chinese Lattice Designs.* New York: Dover Publications, Inc., 1974.

Edwards, Edward B. *Pattern and Design with Dynamic Symmetry.* New York: Dover Publications, Inc., 1967.

Euclides. *The Thirteen Books of Euclid's Elements.* Translated from the text of Heiberg, 2nd edition. New York: Dover Publications, Inc., 1956.

Ghyka, Matila. *The Geometry of Art and Life.* New York: Dover Publications, Inc., 1977.

Graves, Maitland. *The Art of Color and Design.* York, PA: The Maple Press Co., 1941.

Hambidge, Jay. Elements of Dynamic Symmetry. New York: Dover Publications, Inc., 1967.

Heath, T.L. Apollonius of Perga, Treatise on Conic Sections. New York: Barnes and Noble, Inc., 1961.

————, *The Works of Archimedes.* New York: Dover Publications, Inc.

Holmes, James M.S.A. *Manuscript Notes on Weaving.* Tunstede, 212 Vaughn's Gap Road, Nashville, TN 37205, 1985.

Itten, Johannes. *Design and Form,* revised edition. New York: Van Nostrand Reinhold Co., 1975.

Kahlenberg, Mary Hunt and Berlant, Anthony. *The Navajo Blanket.* Praeger Publishers, Inc. in association with the Los Angeles County Museum of Art, 1972.

Kepes, Gyorgy, *Education of Vision.* New York: George Braziller, 1965.

————, *Module, Proportions, Symmetry, Rhythm.* New York: George Braziller, 1966.

Ouchi, Hajima. *Japanese Optical and Geometrical Art.* New York: Dover Publications, Inc., 1973.

Pauly, Sarah B. and Corrie, Rebecca W. *The Kashmir Shawl.* (exhibition catalog). New Haven: Yale University Art Gallery, 1975.

Petrie, Flinders. *Decorative Patterns of the Ancient World for Craftsmen.* New York: Dover Publications, Inc., 1974.

Proctor, Richard M. *The Principles of Pattern.* New York: Van Nostrand Reinhold Co., 1969.

Rossbach, Ed. *The Art of Paisley.* New York: Van Nostrand Reinhold Co., 1980.

Upjohn, Everard M.; Wingert, Paul S.; and Mahler, Jane Gaston. *History of World Art,* 2nd edition. Oxford University Press, 1958.

Whiteford, Andrew Hunter. *North American Indian Arts.* New York: Golden Press, 1970.

Wong, Wucius. *Principles of Two-Dimensional Design.* New York: Van Nostrand Reinhold Co., 1972.

Weaving

Anderson, Clarita; Gordon, Judith; and Towner, Naomi Whiting. *Weave Structures Used in North American Coverlets.* Olney, MD: Clarita Anderson, 1979.

Atwater, Mary Meigs. *Byways in Handweaving.* New York: The Macmillan Co., 1954.

————, *The Shuttle-Craft Book of American Handweaving.* revised edition. New York: Macmillan Co., 1969.

Baizerman, Suzanne and Searles, Karen. *Finishes in the Ethnic Tradition.* St. Paul, MN: Dos Tejedoras, 1978.

————, *Latin American Brocades: Explorations in Supplementary Weft Techniques.* St. Paul, MN: Dos Tejedoras, 1976.

Birrell, Verla. *The Textile Arts.* New York: Schocken, 1973.

Burnham, Harold B. and Burnham, Dorothy K. *Keep Me Warm One Night: Early Handweaving in Eastern Canada.* Toronto, Canada: University of Toronto Press, 1972.

Davidson, Marguerite Porter. *A Handweaver's Pattern Book.* Swarthmore, PA: Marguerite Davison 1951, 1966.